SHUT UP LEGS!

SHUT UP LEGS!

JENS VOIGT

WITH JAMES STARTT

1 3 5 7 9 10 8 6 4 2

Ebury Press, an imprint of Ebury Publishing
20 Vauxhall Bridge Road
London SW1V 2SA

Ebury Press is part of the Penguin Random House group of companies
whose addresses can be found at global.penguinrandomhouse.com

First published in by Ebury Press in 2016
First published in the USA by Rodale 2016

www.eburypublishing.co.uk

A CIP catalogue record for this book is available from the British Library

ISBN 9781785031731

Printed and bound in Great Britain by Clays Ltd, St Ives PLC

Penguin Random House is committed to a sustainable future
for our business, our readers and our planet. This book is
made from Forest Stewardship Council® certified paper.

Contents

CAF 1991

Introduction

"There could be land mines anywhere!"

AND THEN THERE WAS A KNOCK ON MY DOOR. I was just sitting there doing homework in my dormitory at the sports high school in East Berlin when friends came in saying, "Hey, the Wall is open! You want to go see what's on the other side?" That was November 9, 1989. I was just 17 at the time, but somehow I knew that my life was about to change forever.

Of course, I knew that there was another world out there, another world besides the one in East Germany. And even though the leaders and the state media always insisted that they built the Wall to protect us, we all knew that mostly it was just holding us back.

I, like just about any German, will never forget that night. Some people were actually afraid to step across and go into West Berlin. But that wasn't a problem for me! Off I went to Invalidenstrasse, like Checkpoint Charlie, one of the three crossings where the Berlin Wall was open that first night. And that's where I saw the West for the first time. As soon as I stepped across, I couldn't believe my eyes! A whole other world just opened up before me. There was more chocolate on the candy rack in one store than I had seen in my whole entire life. And everything was just so clean! West Berlin was so much cleaner than where I had grown up in East Berlin. Everything, it seemed, was bigger and better. And everything was newer. Everything was well maintained.

You could tell immediately that there was more money there. It was a new world. It was truly UNBELIEVABLE!

But at the same time, the whole event was weird. I was nervous. Let's not forget that I'd had 17 years of brainwashing behind me, 17 years of people telling me that where I now stood—the capitalist West—was enemy territory. I had been taught to believe that in the West, somebody was always ready to steal my wallet. Like I said, we had been told that the Iron Curtain was there to protect us from the "Evil West." Nobody told us that the Iron Curtain was there to keep us inside! So for the first couple of hours, at least, we really had the feeling that there could actually be land mines anywhere! It was a very strange, very singular moment, when we were fascinated but also well aware that we were not in our home country. It was uncomfortable in many ways, and you couldn't let down your guard. But boy, was it exciting!

For hours, days, even weeks afterward, we half expected that the authorities would just close the Wall back up again and say, "Okay, you saw what was on the other side, but that's it! Get back to your real lives!" Honestly, it took a good year until East and West Germany were officially reunited, before we understood that the Wall was down forever. Until then, we just thought that the Russians could show up at any moment and shut things down again.

And even today, I often think back to that night and what my life was like before. Such things are still very much with me.

You know, today people often ask me, "So what's it like being Jens Voigt?" And when I think about it, even after two decades as a professional athlete on several of the world's best cycling teams, I think a lot of it goes back to the days when I was living in a Communist country. It was a unique experience growing up in old East Germany. And to be very honest, it has served me well in life.

I know that may sound strange today, but growing up in East Germany was really great. It was a great place for kids—very safe—and there was a lot of support for us. Life was centered on the common good, the collective. It was much less individualistic than life in a capitalist country, so I learned to be a team player at a young age, which served me well in my career as a cyclist. But I was fortunate to be able to eventually turn professional and work with some of the greatest teams in the sport once the Wall came down, an opportunity that a lot of my countrymen before me never had. That said, a lot of the things I learned growing up helped me have a long and successful career. Because I had much more of a career than I could ever have dreamed of, I never took it for granted. Quite the opposite, it inspired me to keep working hard to simply continue doing what I loved, which was riding bikes.

And now people even come up to me wearing T-shirts featuring quotes of mine, like "Shut up, legs!" I go to the bike shows, and people come up and ask me, "Say it! Come on, Jens. Tell us what we want to hear!" And I say it again: "Shut up, legs!" People love it.

It was just a quote I once said to a journalist asking me how I could dig so deep. But it resonates. People respond to the attitude I bring to the sport. It surprises me, but yes, I'm also flattered. I'm proud. For me, this kind of attention is one of the highest compliments I can receive, because apparently it means that I inspire people! And how many people can say such a thing, that they actually inspire others or maybe change people's lives just a little? That idea alone is worth more than all the trophies and jerseys I've collected over the years.

Yet it's a feeling that also brings a lot of responsibility. It's still sort of a surprise to me, because I was never aiming for such things. I've just been myself, and people always know what I think because I speak frankly and honestly, while still trying not to step on the toes of others.

After a while, I guess people just started to notice and say to themselves, "Hey, look at that! Jens walks a straight line. There are no bad stories, no scandals. He's always reliable. He's always there. You can count on him!"

And let's not forget that my funny German accent helps a bit as well! I can only guess why I have become popular, but I think it has something to do with all those things.

People see what they get with me, and they get what they see. I don't pretend. I don't have brilliant earrings. I don't have tattoos. I don't have a Porsche or Ferrari in my garage. It's just me. I didn't grow up in a materialistic culture. Yet maybe that's what connects. There's so much crisis in the world. And throughout my entire career, it seems, there have been big problems in our sport. Things are moving and changing so fast, and maybe people see some sort of stability in me. I'm sort of like a rock in the ocean. The waves are crashing against me, but I just stand there, unmoved. There is a lot of risk in life, and there are so many scandals and disappointments in sports, so I think people respond well to the stable factor that I bring to the table.

I don't know what it is exactly, but I can say one thing: All this attention provided serious motivation for me toward the end of my career and helped contribute to its longevity.

It was an amazing ride, really, and I still pinch myself sometimes when I think back on the road I've traveled. I won more races than I ever thought possible, but just as important, I traveled to more places than I ever thought possible and met more kinds of people than I ever thought possible. And all this time, that little East German village boy has still been inside me, his eyes wide open in amazement.

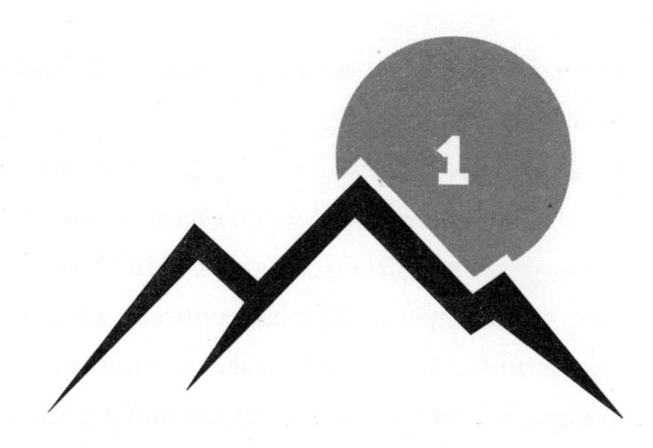

GROWING UP IN EAST GERMANY

"While the Communist system sometimes looked good on paper, unfortunately, it was run by human beings."

"JUST DON'T SHOOT ME IN THE BACK! You can run, but whatever you do, don't shoot me!"

That's what my father, Egon, would tell his patrol partner every night as a young soldier in the East German army. My dad was born in 1946 and was one of the first kids born into the new East Germany, established when the country was divided at the end of World War II. And even though East Germany and West Germany were two separate states throughout most of his childhood, the borders remained open.

It was not until they started building the Wall in 1961 that people were confronted with absolute choices, and some would flee desperately to the West. This is exactly when my dad was serving his military duty. Now when we talk about the Wall, most people just think about the

Berlin Wall. But that was only a small piece of it. In reality, a whole barrier system was set up all along the border with West Germany.

You see, back in the early days of Communism, back when they were still building the Wall, soldiers always went out on patrol in pairs. Part of the logic was that they were supposed to sort of patrol each other, as well. And if one of the soldiers made a break for it, to try to flee to the West, the other was expected to shoot.

And since Dassow, where my dad lived, was next to the West German border by the Baltic Sea, a lot of soldiers would try to flee. The problem with this patrol method, though, was that if a soldier was going to make a run for it, often he would shoot his partner first, so that the partner could not shoot him when he ran.

Night after night, my dad would just make it clear to his partner that he wouldn't shoot, so there was no reason for his partner to get paranoid and shoot him first. Pretty crazy! But then those were crazy times.

My dad was like most Germans, who are themselves like most other people. And like most other people, if you give them the choice to live wherever they want, the vast majority will choose to stay right where they are. My dad was like that. He wasn't going to run, but he didn't want to get shot for staying in East Germany, either!

And although my childhood in East Germany is more and more a part of my past, as I have said, it still remains very much a part of me. It's funny. When you add them up, those years amount to less than half of my life now. But they were formative years, spent in an entirely different world than what my children know today.

Like most others, I try to erase the bad memories from my past and focus instead on the positive ones. And that's why all these years later, there still aren't too many bad things I can say about growing up in East Germany.

Basically, I had a good, happy childhood, one with no stress. Life was just slower. It was lived on a smaller scale than life today. And it was more relaxed. Part of the reason for that was that Dassow was such a small town. I remember back in 1987, we celebrated the 50th anniversary of Dassow's first receiving official "city" status. Up until then, it was officially considered just a village. I thought, "Huh? You mean this little town is officially big enough to be considered a city?" It still looked pretty small to me! Up until then, I just never saw Dassow as anything more than a village, because, well, it really is.

Growing up, I spent most of my time outside. But even then it seemed as though 20 to 30 steps in either direction would take me out of the village. That's how small it appeared through the eyes of even a child. We had one shoe shop, one clothing shop, one flower shop, one toy store, one newsstand and stationery shop, one food shop, and one bakery. That was about it. Now part of that was simply a result of living in Communist East Germany. There was never any market competition, so we just had one shop to supply each of our basic needs. But part of it was also just Dassow.

None of that could keep me from dreaming big dreams, though. My first great dream was to become an astronaut. Flying into space was just the biggest adventure I could imagine. The dream was fueled by East German television, which documented Soviet flights and the adventures of Sigmund Jähn, an East German, who became the first German to enter outer space when he joined the Soviet Intercosmos mission in 1976. Jähn was such a hero, I imagine most East German kids at the time wanted to be astronauts.

Soon, however, I decided that space might not be my thing and I would be better off as a forestry engineer, because I loved the great outdoors so much. That dream lasted until I entered a special sports high school in Berlin, where I quickly realized that it would be hard to spend my life in the forest if I was going to become a world-class athlete.

Once I got into the high school system, I thought journalism might be the best career path. I'd always loved reading, and if you can believe it, I was even in the poetry club for a while. I also enjoyed writing, so the idea of working for one of the news agencies was appealing to me. But once the Wall came down, everything changed.

Before the Wall came down, life was just so much simpler and more relaxed. The Communist system did its best to eliminate competition. There was no stress about careers, no stress about outperforming somebody else. For the average person, there wasn't a big difference in status among different professions. You have to remember that in East Germany, an engineer, a doctor, or a factory worker like my dad pretty much all made the same salary. Egon worked as a metallurgist for a company making farm equipment, and my mom, Edith, was one of the town's photographers.

Egon was the big one in the family. He is tall like me and as strong as an ox. But he was quiet, too, quite unlike me! As a kid, he was a pretty good soccer player, but he never really had the chance to pursue sports because of his responsibilities on the family farm. And once he was older, most of his strength was put to good use working in the factory.

To be honest, I didn't see all that much of my dad when I was growing up, because he generally left for work before I got up in the morning. He would come home at 4:30 or 5:00 p.m. Sometimes we did homework with him, but I came to realize that when he came home from work most days, he was just exhausted.

I saw more of my mom. Edith was able to arrange her work so that she pretty much only worked half days. That way she could tend to us three kids. She would get up with us in the morning, fix us breakfast, and then go off to work. After school, we would often meet her at the photo studio and start doing our homework while she finished up. Then we would all go home together.

My parents didn't have big, important jobs, but they only made, say, 100 marks (about 50 US dollars) less per month than a doctor did. And it wasn't a competitive thing, either, because everybody knew they weren't going to get rich anytime soon. This acceptance led to far less jealousy among people than you see today, because, well, people had a lot less to be jealous of. As a result, I do think that people were friendlier to each other back then. They just had a lot more time to spend in their gardens talking to their friends, having a barbecue, or kicking a ball around.

Also, although it might be hard to imagine today, consumerism basically didn't exist back in East Germany. For starters, our choices of brands and products were very limited. Motorbikes were all MZ. Televisions were Strassfurth. Cameras were all Praktica. It was the same for just about everything: radios, bread, sugar, you name it.

There were only two types of cars: a big one and a small one! The Trabant was the small car and Wartburg was the big car, so people weren't obsessed with the make, model, or size of their cars.

And like just about everything else except food, cars were really hard to get in East Germany. They were so hard to get that, believe it or not, the standard procedure was that when a child was born, his or her parents would register the baby for a car! That way, when the child was 16 or 17, it would be their turn on the waiting list and they would get one.

My parents were regular working-class people with three kids: my older brother, Ronny; me; and my sister, Cornelia. We never had much money, and we didn't get our first car until I was about 15. But that said, we had what we needed.

In some ways, growing up in Dassow was different from growing up in most other parts of the country, because our village was located on the border of East Germany and West Germany. As a result, we were more aware of the differences between the two cultures than most other East Germans were. Heck, if we turned our antennas in the right direction, we could even get West German radio and television! But we had to be careful that the police didn't see which way the antennas pointed, or there could be a knock on the door!

Nevertheless, we had few regrets about living in East Germany. My dad had made a life for himself in Dassow. That's where he came from. That's where he met Edith. That's where he had his children. That's where he had a job. He never had a reason to be unhappy. Really, when I think back on my parents, they were always very grounded, and they kept things in perspective.

Although they never tried to flee East Germany, they didn't embrace the Communist system, either, and refused to become members of the party. There were consequences for such decisions! It definitely cost my father certain jobs, and I can tell you that it didn't look good on my application to sports school later on, either. But Egon always said, "Jens, shortcuts in life just give you short-term advantages. Be true to who you are."

My father also understood that if he ever did cross the border, he would be a nobody. He would have to start over again, and it was not a given that his life would be better, that he was going to make big money or anything. Plenty of people were actually worse off after crossing.

I remember how, when the Wall came down, people were saying, "Well, now we have the freedom, but we don't have the money to express that freedom!" And they were right. Sure, in theory, they had the freedom to suddenly pick up and go to Hawaii, but they didn't necessarily have the money to buy the plane tickets!

So once the Wall came down, all of us East Germans quickly realized that there was potential for life to be better, but not for everybody. There was a lot more stress, and we had a lot more responsibility for ourselves. We had to work hard.

In East Germany, you really didn't have to work hard at all. It was just a no-go that you could get fired. There was no unemployment in East Germany. Can you imagine that today? Even if you were lazy or just plain stupid, the state would create a job for you. That was definitely one of the advantages of the Communist system.

But while the Communist system sometimes looked good on paper, unfortunately, it was run by human beings. And so, inevitably, it just went to shit! That's the way it is with us people. The idea was that everybody would work as hard as he could for the common good. You know, just out of their own good conscience and goodwill, everyone would strive to be better. The stronger would unite to pull the weaker up. It's a beautiful idea in theory, but it just didn't turn out that way.

And, of course, life wasn't all good. It was filled with propaganda and surveillance, and the state really controlled individual lives. Officially, it was illegal to listen to West German radio stations or watch movies from the West, although we did have access to certain authorized films, books, or music. Now my parents were pretty relaxed about it and would let us watch the movies coming directly from the West. But we had to promise not to talk about it in school the next day. Like I said, if those radio and television antennas were pointed in the wrong direction—toward the West—the police would show up at your door. Often, we just had to point the antennas to the eastern side, even though we knew that western reception would not be as good, because if your antenna was pointed east, it was impossible to get good reception from the west.

It was pretty scary, really. Heck, I remember one day, maybe 10 years after the Wall came down, my dad was listening to Radio Hamburg and working in the garage. All of a sudden, a police car drove by, and my dad just jumped! It was pure reflex. "Oh my God!" he said. "Can you believe that after all these years I'm still afraid to listen to the wrong radio station?" Can you imagine how much fear had been burned into his brain? How strong the control and the fear were? "I have to laugh at myself," he said. "But I'm just shocked at how deeply it's still inside me!"

On days when we had state elections, the police would show up at our door if we didn't vote before noon. I remember my grandma,

Frieda. She was a bit of a rebel. And she would just forget about the elections. She was strong, just tough as nails, and she was always working on the farm. She would be busy feeding her chickens or something, and the police would come and take her to vote! Frieda also had three sisters living in West Germany, and although she was pressured to cut the ties, she always refused and continued to correspond with them even though that, too, was not looked upon well. Mail did circulate between the two countries, and we always got letters or Christmas boxes from our relatives in West Germany, although I'm sure they were opened and read by some customs officer prior to delivery.

But my grandma told it like it was. I remember in school they taught us that after the Wall went up, all the farmers just donated all their equipment to the collective. But Frieda told us otherwise. "Oh no," she said. "They [the state] just came at three in the morning and took it all away! They didn't ask us anything. They just came and took everything away!"

You know, it took me until I was 22 to understand that Hitler and Stalin had signed a nonaggression pact and split up Poland during World War II. That's not what we learned in school! In East Germany, they taught us that Hitler attacked Poland and the good, wise Stalin went into the eastern side of Poland to save as many Polish people as he could from the hands of the Nazis. What they didn't tell us was that when the Nazi and Russian troops finally came together in central Poland, they held victory parades together and basically chopped the country in two and shared the spoils of their success. No, they didn't teach us *that* in school!

It wasn't until well after the Wall came down, until my own kids were actually in school themselves, that I learned things were quite different. I remember going to the library, reading up on what really happened in World War II, and just being astonished. They lied to a whole generation!

One thing I have learned from all this, however, is that the winners write the history books. That's the way it is in life. That's the way it is in cycling, for that matter. And when I was growing up in East Germany, the winner was Communism!

So, obviously, not everything was great in East Germany. And looking back, I think in some ways I was quite lucky, because I had some sympathetic teachers. The fact that my parents weren't card-carrying members of the Communist Party and we had family in West Germany didn't win me any favors in the state sports school. And already, as a young kid, little "Jensie" would also say whatever came into his head and speak his mind.

But, fortunately, my homeroom teacher, Dieter Richnow, took a liking to me and was aware that the truth was not exactly what was being taught in school. I would say, "Ah no! My grandma says that the state just came and took away the tools!" Of course, he couldn't officially agree with me and in class had to say things like, "Ah no, the state would never do something like that!" But he didn't report me or anything. If he had, they could have just sent me home! Game over!

But like I said, what I remember most about life in East Germany was how relaxed it was at the time. At least when it came to stress levels, the old system was pretty successful, because, well, there was a lot less stress. And that had a lasting impact on how I later viewed my financial situation as a professional.

Maybe I could have become richer, for example, by being more tenacious or by changing teams more often. But I've always been happy with where I've been, and as a professional cyclist, I've basically been happy with the amount of money I've been making at any given time. Sure, I probably missed some opportunities to make more money. But those opportunities generally bring with them more stress, which I've always tried to avoid.

And that comes back to my upbringing, because when it comes to money, I have always been of the mind that if I'm making enough, why do I need more? It's like, how many beds do you need to sleep in? Why would I need a house with 15 bedrooms?

Materialism really only came to me later in life when I had kids, because having six kids in a city such as Berlin forced me to be more aware of money. The cost of living for six children has a way of imposing financial concerns on you. So the days when I could just float along were long over. Yet even with the pressures of supporting a family, I've always tried to keep finances in perspective. I wanted to make decent money, sure, but not at the expense of time with my family.

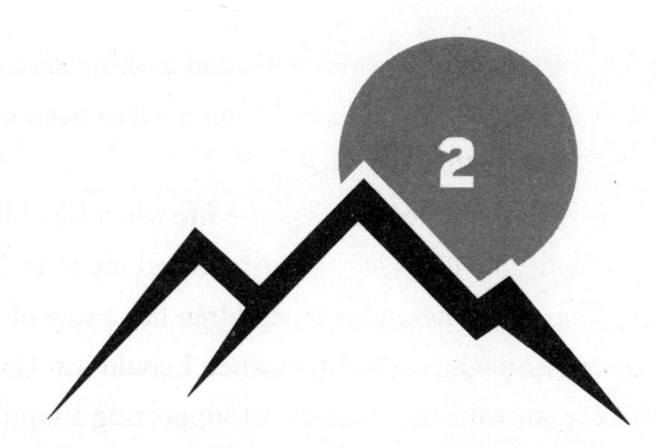

STARTING CYCLING

"I owe it all to the pigs!"

Jens as seen by Jan Schaffrath (schoolmate of Voigt's, former professional cyclist, Etixx–Quick-Step team director):

I've known Jens since he was eight or nine years old. We were born on the same exact day, the same exact year, so in some ways, we were like brothers when we were growing up in East Germany. We both started out in long-distance running, and at a very young age, we would be fighting it out for victory in cross-country races. And then a couple of years later, we ran into each other at the sports school and became really good friends.

At first, sports school was really hard for him. He came from the country and was all alone in Berlin, and he really missed his parents. Me, I lived in Berlin, so I went home at the end of the day, unlike Jens, who lived in the dormitory. So my family kind of took him in, especially that first year, and he often would come home with me.

That first year, he really struggled just to keep his spot at the school. It was really competitive, and sometimes fights would break out. I just kept encouraging him, because I knew that he was stronger than most of the guys there, and sure enough, at the end of the year, Jens made the cut, while some of the others were sent home. He just wanted it more!

When I see him today, I often think back on the years when we were growing up. And the one thing that never changed with Jens was his desire to win. It didn't matter if it was cross-country, soccer, or cycling—he always wanted to win! I'll never forget that. At the sports school, we played a lot of soccer in the winter. And Jens always played to win. He was far from the best player on a technical level, but he was just running nonstop all over the field, trying to make a play. He just wouldn't give up. It didn't matter if we were four goals behind. Jens did not know how to give up. Defeat just was not part of his vocabulary. And it still isn't today!

LIKE JUST ABOUT EVERY GERMAN BOY, I PLAYED SOCCER FIRST. But I lacked hand-eye coordination, which is kind of important in that sport. And I certainly wasn't good enough to dribble around defenders and score goals, which is pretty much all boys want to do when they first start out. If I wanted to be easy on myself, I would say I was just hopeless! But being awful at soccer did have one hidden benefit. It helped steer me toward endurance sports, which, as you know, I was pretty good at!

Not that I knew it at the time, of course. No, at nine years old, all that I, or anybody close to me, knew was that without soccer, I had way too much time on my hands. And way too much energy to burn!

I, of course, thought I was being funny and creative when, for example, I tried to ride a local farmer's sheep like a horse. I felt like John Wayne!

At the time, pirate movies and westerns were our favorite movies to watch when West German TV reception was good. But we couldn't talk about them in school because they were strictly forbidden. Are you kidding, John Wayne and Communism? No, they simply did not mix. Standing up for yourself the way Wayne did. Taking justice into his own hands. No, that is not what East German authorities wanted to promote!

Little misadventures, such as riding the farmer's sheep, did not amuse my teachers or my parents, and just plain got me in a lot of trouble. In the eyes of my teachers I was just too energetic. So one day, my homeroom teacher came to my parents and said, "Listen, your son has way too much energy! He has to find some sport to burn it off. He just has to!" Now, back in the day, they called me a wild child. Today they have another name for it. They would have diagnosed me with ADD in a split second, bounced me from therapy to therapy, and prescribed me drugs until I seemed normal.

In East Germany, however, there just wasn't that kind of personalized attention. Instead, running became my medicine. Right away, I found that I was pretty good at running medium and long distances and immediately started winning local races and placing in bigger events. Without cycling, I would definitely have been a 5,000- or 10,000-meter runner.

My track-and-field career came to a premature end, however, when I failed to meet the desired objective in a long-jump test one day. My coach, convinced that I was not giving my all, punished me by making me run laps. And, with each lap, my anger just mounted and mounted, and finally I quit and never returned.

Looking back on it now, I still think I was right. I mean, how many times have you heard "Jensie" get criticized for not giving his all? I just don't do that! That's just not me. And that attitude was instilled very early on, because my dad hammered it into me. "Son," he'd say, "if you're going to do something, then do it all the way!" Egon was all about dispensing old-school wisdom, and he was about as old school as it gets. "Boys don't cry!" That was another. And it worked on me, because since I've grown up, only one thing has made me cry—the birth of my children!

Soon enough, I was looking for another sport. And one day, the cycling club BSK Traktor Dassow showed up at my school, the POS Ernst Puchmüller—named inevitably after some anti-Fascist from World War II. The coach gave a little presentation about the cycling team. And even better than that, they offered these brand-new metallic silver racing bikes to everybody who would sign up the same afternoon.

And hey, if you're an almost-10-year-old boy from a simple working-class family and somebody offers you a brand-new free bike, what can you say besides "Hell yeah, I want to sign up!"?

A free racing bike? That was so awesome! And I will never forget the brand. It was Diamant. But that's easy to remember, because it was the only bike company we had in East Germany.

So there I was with my new Diamant. I couldn't have been any happier. Obviously, at that age, I knew nothing about Gitane, Pinarello, or any other bike manufacturer, really. I was just happy to have my own bike to ride. After a few weeks of training, we did our first race, the state championship uphill time trial. It was held about 200 kilometers east of Dassow. And I won!

It's funny, though, because when I think back on it today, what I remember most about it is not the race itself, but the fact that I had to wait until I got home before I could tell my parents. Why, you wonder? Well, for the simple reason that we didn't have a phone. Of course, this was well before the age of the Internet and mobile telephones. But damn, my parents didn't even have a landline!

In those first years, when I was 10 or 11 years old, I honestly think I won every single race I started, save maybe the national championships. I was just stronger than the other boys. I would go to the front, and nobody could follow. When I was 12, I still won, say, three-quarters of the races. Sports were fun. It was just like a game. Soon enough, I was invited to try out for one of the elite national sports schools, a huge opportunity for any kid in East Germany, because sports played a huge role in Communist society.

But then, in 1984, some strange pig disease, Maul-und-Klauenseuche, spread throughout the area, and the entire town of Dassow got quarantined! It sounds funny to talk about this today, but the pig disease actually played a huge role in my career. Suddenly, I couldn't train. Suddenly, I lost all my fitness because of it. We couldn't leave town, and the authorities really didn't even want us playing sports in town. The only problem was that the pig disease came at about the same time I was taking the tests to get into the sports school. I did manage to pass the test, but I wasn't as good as I had been. And all of a sudden, I really had to work!

So there was little "Jensie," this 14-year-old kid going to the KJS Ernst Grube sports school in Berlin. Just about every school in East Germany was named after some martyr who died at the hand of the Nazi regime, and Ernst was one of them.

Berlin was the big city, and leaving home for the first time when I was just 14 was not easy. It was the first time I had seen buildings higher than two or three stories, and in my eyes, that was a pretty big deal. And there were a lot of changes. I was the youngest student at the boarding school. And, of course, all the older kids were telling me where my place was in the pecking order. Back in Dassow, I was one of the leaders in the school, because I was a good student, and I was good in sports. But in Berlin, I was no leader! It wasn't easy. I was getting into fights and also getting worn down with studying and training all the time. At the same time, my body was growing.

And the result of all this was that it was a difficult time for me. All of a sudden I was just managing to get by, to pass the tests each year—to do the required times in time trialing, and so on. So I wasn't as good as I had been, and that was hard for me to accept.

The way cycling was structured, there was no sports school in the northern region where I came from. So we had to compete with the kids from all around Berlin. And it was very competitive! After the first test, only 45 kids were left, and after the second, only about 30 kids. Then they sent us to this sort of nationwide mini-Olympics in Dresden, and only 10 to 15 kids from each region were selected to compete. They tested not only our cycling but also our general athletic strength and went so far as to do these sophisticated morphology tests to predict how our bodies would mature physically in the coming years. Those tests actually helped me, because I was a late developer. Some kids were already shaving at the age of 14. Not me! Because these tests were based on a sort of curve that took into account your current level of maturity, I was able to score points against kids who were simply more developed physically.

So I made the cut, and in 1984, I was sent off to sports school. But sports weren't just games anymore. And suddenly, I had to work very hard just to keep up. I had to really work, really sacrifice, then go get my head kicked in. Then I had to go back to the start line and get my head kicked in again. It was tough, but the experience taught me a lot about sacrifice and suffering, two things that have come in handy throughout my career.

I often think that the sports school was my own school for suffering. As I said, I had to struggle just to survive, so I think that over all these years, I learned to set my pain threshold higher than other people's. After doing just that for 15 or 20 years, well, I think I have a pain threshold that is 10 to 20 percent higher than most others. I don't know if you can scientifically prove it, but I totally believe it. It makes sense to me. That's the way I feel. By just repeating the level of suffering, the body goes, "Okay, I know how this feels. Now go farther."

You also see the world differently when you're down. When you're down a little bit, there are always people who will kick you. But other people will reach out to you and say, "Hey, let me give you a helping hand. I can help you out of this." And in moments like that, you discover who is true, who is false, who is a friend, and who is just a wannabe friend.

One of my best friends at the time was Jan Schaffrath. He was my age. But he was a superhero of the sports school. Ah, he was just so good. Unbelievable! He could time trial. He won road races. He won on the track. He was superfast and could beat professionals such as Olaf Ludwig or Erik Zabel while he was still an amateur. He was just a huge talent. And he was my friend! He was a good friend to have, because he really stuck up for me when it came to bullying. And as a result, I often worked for him. We have remained friends for life. After racing for Team Telekom and Milram, he has gone on to be a successful team director. He's a great rider and a great guy!

Was it a hard period? Yes! Geez, I was just 14 years old when I started. I was missing home and at the same time seeing some of my friends go home and quit. We lost the first kid after just a month. And another went home for Christmas and didn't come back.

It was just a very hard time for me. For the first 14 years of my life, I had lived pretty much a pressure-free existence. And all of a sudden, I was surrounded by pressure. Sports school was all about making the grade, about being good enough, something I'd never once questioned before.

In addition, I had grown up in a very harmonious family. I wasn't used to being all alone. And because I was spending so much time training, my grades suffered. But I kept telling myself, "No, no, you can't go home!" My parents loved me and always said I could come home. But I also knew that they were proud of me and where I was going. They never put pressure on me, but I really didn't want to let them down. The result was that already at the age of 14 or 15, I was confronted with my first make-or-break moment.

To be honest, there were definitely some points when I thought about throwing in the towel. But, fortunately, I had some good friends who were there for me, and I learned a lot about myself and really grew as a person. And it wasn't like I could just pick up and go home, either. My parents didn't have a car at the time—they were still waiting to receive their first one—and they lived 300 kilometers away. So it wasn't like I could go home crying whenever I wanted. No, I just had me!

Things started to improve after that first year, but in those first years in the sports school, I learned that you need a team to succeed . . . that you can't always be the strongest, and that sports, like life, are about taking and giving. Now this happened to coincide perfectly with everything they were teaching us in school about the *kollektiv*, the collective, which was about taking and giving so that the stronger help the weaker. Nobody was saying, "If you're going to have a career, then you've got to use your elbows." That sort of mentality just didn't exist!

The old sports school system also taught me how to deal with pressure, because like I said, it was always there. We were always being tested. And being selected was no pleasure cruise. All it meant was that I was going to be tested again and again. In the beginning, nearly 150 kids entered the program from all around the country, but by the time they got done with the elimination process, only about 15 riders qualified. So you really had no choice but to get used to working under pressure.

Yet while the East German system was very much based on working for the common good, the bike taught me the need to also fend for myself. Individualism, of course, was not part of the East German mentality, but something strange happened to me on a bike that made me question such ideas, because when I was in my third year of sports school, I won my first road race. Ironically, it was a race in which I was the only member of my team present. How crazy is that? That was a huge event for me, and it made me question a lot about myself and what I had been taught. I'd won some time trials previously, but this was a road race. I realized in that race that there were no safety nets. There was no one else to save the situation but myself. There was no coach telling me what to do, what to eat, when to attack. It was at that race that I first understood that once I took things into my own hands, I was a lot better than I thought. I'll never forget that race. The weather was shitty all day, and in the final, there were only about 25 guys left. I was looking for the right moment, and finally I attacked about 3 kilometers from the finish. I just went full gas, and I won.

I was ecstatic, of course, but it was bizarre, too, because I did it alone. It was strange. Were my teammates just bringing me down? That thought did enter my mind. But mostly it just gave me a lot of confidence in myself. I realized that I didn't have to be a follower, that if I believed in myself, things could work out, too! Because I didn't win straightaway when I arrived at KJS Ernst Grube, I'd become much more of a worker, just doing what people told me. But from then on, I raced with a lot more self-confidence.

Nothing came easy in sports school, but the lessons I learned there served me well once I turned professional. I often say, in fact, that I had the best of both worlds.

Sports, of course, were superimportant in East Germany, and the school system worked closely with the sports system to find and develop talent. It was a very, very expansive system, and in many ways very successful. Obviously, we've learned, looking back, that it was a deeply flawed system, rife with doping. That said, we have learned in recent years that the other side was not much better, as doping among the West German teams has been widely reported. In retrospect, the Olympics were really nothing more than a clash of the titans.

Nevertheless, the East German system was very successful in its ability to identify and develop talent from a young age. And that aspect of the sports system has remained in place in Germany even today, long after the collapse of Communism.

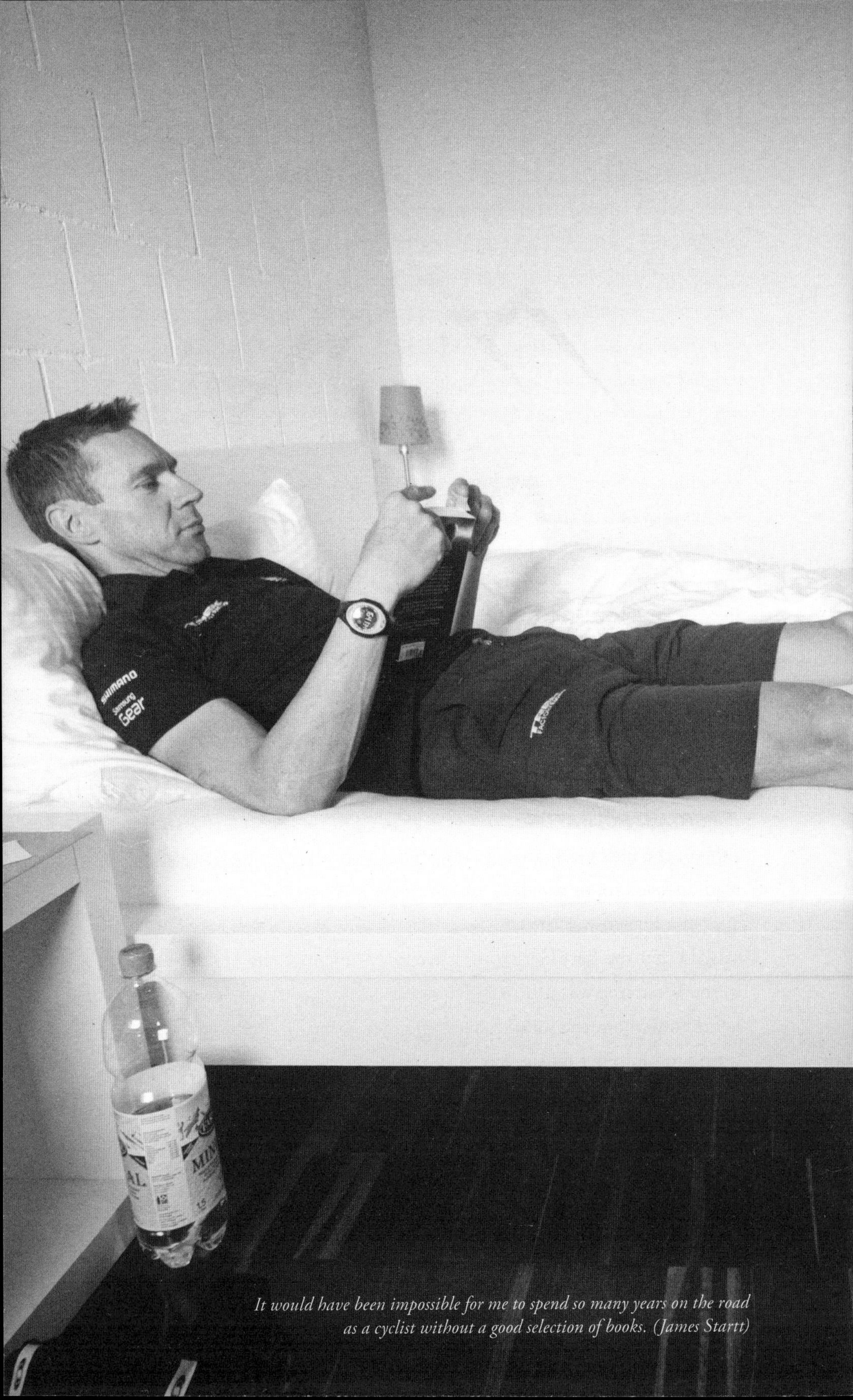

It would have been impossible for me to spend so many years on the road as a cyclist without a good selection of books. (James Startt)

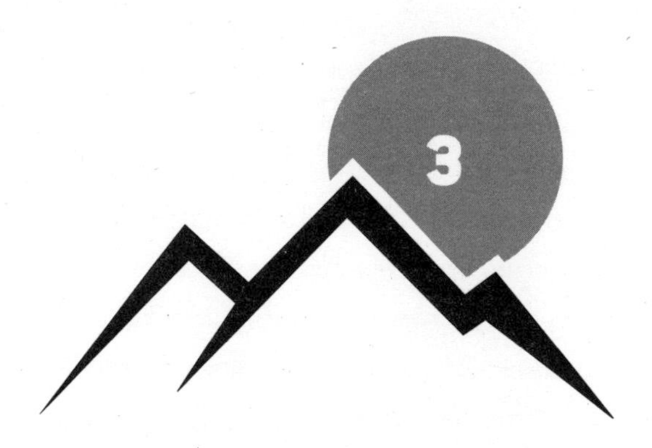

READING

"I want to open a bookstore where I am
my own best customer."

FOR MOST KIDS GROWING UP, BOOKS, MUSIC, AND MOVIES PLAY AN IMPORTANT ROLE AT ONE POINT OR ANOTHER. I was no exception, even though the East German government censored everything that we read, listened to, or watched.

Nina Hagen was the enfant terrible of the German scene. She was so wild that the East Germans were actually happy to let her out to go to the West. She was just so different, so crazy, that people knew about her even without the social media outlets of today. To be honest, I wasn't too into her music, but we sure talked about it a lot.

Some Western groups even made it across the airwaves to us. Duran Duran was just huge, and Madonna and Cyndi Lauper were getting big despite the censorship. That said, "Girls Just Want to Have Fun" never did get played on East German radio!

For me, though, the big band I remember was Karat, as in "14-karat gold." They had a song called "Seven Bridges." It was about someone who was in prison for seven years, and each year he would cross another bridge toward freedom. I guess you could say it was a sort of metaphor for life under Communist rule; I'm not sure. And I'm also not quite sure how it passed censorship, to be honest. But it was a very popular song.

From a very young age, however, reading became a central part of my life, a great pastime as I got more and more involved in sports. It provided a perfect counterbalance.

Like pretty much everyone, I learned to read at the age of 6 or 7, and it just opened an entirely new world to me. I could get absorbed in books and spend hours with them alone in my room.

I loved adventure books by authors such as James Fenimore Cooper. I just loved stories such as *The Last of the Mohicans*. I loved learning about the Indians. And Cooper's books were authorized by the East German authorities because the Indians' struggle against the white man was seen as a sort of struggle against capitalism, and of course, the Communist regime liked anybody who was against capitalism!

And then there was Jack London, probably my all-time favorite writer. He, too, was authorized in East Germany because he was an early supporter of Socialism. And he has at least three books on my all-time favorites list. *White Fang*, *The Call of the Wild*, and *Klondike Tales* are right up there with Hemingway's *The Old Man and the Sea* and *Peeling the Onion* by Günter Grass. As I got older, I also read more challenging books, such as *The Name of the Rose* by Umberto Eco. But I never forgot those adventure novels I read as a kid.

I just loved the simplicity of London's writing. There's always a central figure caught in this amazing struggle to survive against all odds. In order to do so, he can leave nothing to chance. It's actually not unlike what a lot of cyclists go through when trying to get through a hard race such as the Tour de France.

Reading helped me. It was sort of an escape from reality, a dream. And still today, I dream of one day spending a winter in Alaska, out in the wild. The great outdoors just fascinates me. And whenever I go to a hotel that has the Discovery Channel available, I love to watch documentaries about people living in the bush, out in the wild.

In all honesty, I think that the adventurous spirit conveyed in such books had a profound impact on my worldview; you know, the way I look at life, my perspective on things.

I've always had a desire to make my own footprints on the path of life. And as I like to say, if you only follow other people, you never make your own footprints, and nobody ever notices that you've been here.

Those are big words, I know, but yes, I would like to leave something that's bigger than me behind. I'd like to do that, be it by leaving my name in the record books or by having children. Some people build houses or make art, and I've always been looking for my own ways to leave a footprint.

I sometimes joked that when I finally retired from cycling, I wanted to open a bookstore where I would be my own best customer. Now that was never very realistic, because such a venture won't pay the bills for my six kids. But it never stopped me from reading!

Even when we're racing and training a lot, cyclists have a lot of downtime. And I love to use that time reading. Now I know a lot of guys have trouble reading at a bike race because, well, when you're really exhausted, you get kind of "bike dumb." Some guys are just too tired or always thinking about the race. Heck, sometimes after racing really hard, you're barely able to pronounce your name, let alone spell it. But for me, reading has always provided a wonderful release.

A lot of my teammates just looked at me in disbelief with all my books. Every year before the Tour de France, for example, I went to my favorite little bookshops in Berlin—not the Internet, but real bookshops—and bought three books, one for each week of the race. My teammates were always saying, "Wait, isn't that a new book again?" And each time I would just say, "Yeah!"

Now guys like Frank and Andy Schleck were honest and admitted that when they were racing, they couldn't even get beyond the introduction of a book, let alone read an entire book. And they actually tried! They saw that reading helped me relax. So sometimes they would bring books along, too. But they just didn't have the patience or energy during a hectic race to read them. But hey, they were always pretty good at *Guitar Hero*!

That said, there is a real correlation between the difficulty of the race I'm competing in and the difficulty of the book I can read. At a small race, such as the Tour du Poitou-Charentes, for example, I can tackle tough books. That's where I read *Peeling the Onion*. Günter Grass was a former East German writer who won the Nobel Prize in 1999. His books are tremendous, but dense. They would be impossible to read during the Tour de France, for example. There, it's just "books with colorful pages," as my wife, Stephanie, says, basically page-turners. When it comes to page-turners, I've been a big fan of science fiction, conspiracy stories, and thrillers. Page-turners at a bike race are great. You can read 10 pages before you get on a plane, 10 pages on the team bus. I can always find time to read 10 pages.

I was never really the type of rider that always talked about his race and how many watts he pushed around what corner, and what gear ratio he pushed on what descent. Some people can recite every stage winner in the last 10 years of the Tour. That's just mind-blowing. It's so impressive to me. But that is just not me.

For me, cycling was always a great job, but I was also really glad when the day was done. And when it was done, that was exactly what it was—done! After I climbed into the team bus and took a shower, I put my mind on rewind, opened my book, and went back to reading where I left off.

My approach does have its drawbacks. The problem for me was that I never could remember my races. Guys will remember a particular race and say, "Oh man! Do you remember this or that climb? Oh, that was hard!" But I'm just like, "Sorry, no!"

You would think that with 17 Tours de France under my belt, I would know every finish in the Tour. But no, I don't. Okay, I remember Alpe d'Huez and some of the big climbs, but there are plenty I just can't remember. So while sometimes my approach to reading and riding can be an advantage, sometimes it can also be a disadvantage. I mean, it helps me to not be a complete bike nerd. Striving to maintain such a balance may have allowed me to maintain something resembling a normal personality. But it's definitely a disadvantage when I don't know where I'm going in a race!

Standing in front of the high school building of my sports school. (James Startt)

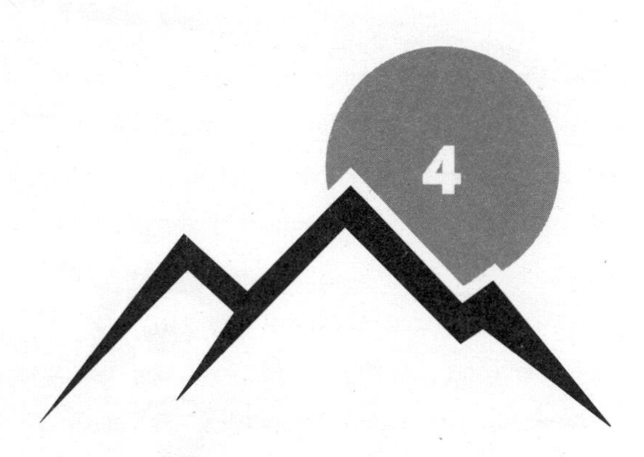

GERMAN UNIFICATION

"It's easy to get lost in the land of abundance!"

AFTER THE WALL CAME DOWN, MY LIFE WAS SUDDENLY FILLED WITH ALL SORTS OF POSSIBILITIES. But it was also filled with questions I'd never asked myself before: questions such as, "How do I make a living racing my bike?"

In East Germany, my life was pretty much spelled out for me. As long as I continued to perform well and get results, I was treated as an elite athlete, a professional basically. Okay, that didn't mean I was going to earn a huge salary or anything, but it would have secured me a four-room apartment—pretty much the biggest apartment available—in Berlin. The state would have given me a car without my waiting for 15 years, and I would have had plenty of money for food and clothes each month.

Once the Wall came down, I suddenly had the capacity to earn far more money than I'd ever dreamed possible. But I also had to figure out how to do it on my own. Somehow I had to be able to get to the races and get the results needed to attract a major professional team to offer me a contract.

For many of us East German athletes, the army provided the best option, because it provided security. So for four-and-a-half years, I was a soldier! Now the army, you have to remember, is one of the most important and valuable sponsors for German sports in general. If you're in the army, you have a job, an official job with social security, retirement benefits, everything. And if you were a member of the special sports school or the German national team, like I was, the military duty was actually minimal. Once a month, I remember, I had to drive to an army base in Frankfurt, change into my army uniform, and stand guard duty for 24 hours. But once that was done, it was back into my cycling uniform and racing my bike! So mostly the army provided me with a practical way to have time to train and race.

And let's not forget the most important part. Back in the day, the German army—and this was important for me—was not a fighting army. With Germany's history in the 20th century, we were pretty much guaranteed not to go into any war. That's not the case anymore. Today the army is voluntary, and they have participated in a lot of military actions: Kosovo, Afghanistan, Mali, and so on. But one reason the German army was an attractive option for some back then was that there was no chance you would be sent into war. In reality, it was just like any other job—well, actually better—because it allowed me to train and race full-time!

I was in the army basically until I signed my first professional contract. But you see, being in the army was the only way to be on the German national team.

Racing for the German national team after the Wall came down gave me my first taste of Western European racing. I did my first

Circuit de la Sarthe and my first Tour du Vaucluse, two good races in France, as well as the PostGiro in Sweden. They were all good races where we had a chance to race against some of the big European professional teams for the first time.

But the highlight for me during all those years was winning the Peace Race with the German national team in 1994.

For old East Germans like me, the Peace Race was the Tour de France! Established after World War II, it was a sort of race of good faith around all the Eastern bloc countries. I mean, let's face it, we Germans had brought so much terror to our neighboring countries in the 20th century that many people in those countries just looked at us like we were all monsters! So in order to rebuild some semblance of normalcy, some semblance of good faith and understanding, we came up with the idea of the Peace Race.

After World War II, people on both sides of the border didn't want to have anything to do with war. All they really wanted to do was to raise their kids in peace, have a job, pay some taxes, see their kids grow up, and see their kids have children. In that regard, the Peace Race was helpful. It brought people together and made them remember that, whatever side of the border they were on, everyone was human. So the Peace Race helped a lot in building good relations after the war, and every year it would go between Poland, Czechoslovakia, East Germany, and Russia. Every year it would start in the capital of one of those countries, go through another, and finish in the capital of yet another. And it always changed so that each country was equally involved. The race symbol was always a white dove, I believe inspired or designed by Picasso, which just goes to show at what level the race was designed to have social significance.

It was a huge race for us, and everything came together for me in 1994. On the first day, I got away in a breakaway with several of the prerace favorites. It was a leg breaker of a stage, I remember, with lots of climbs. I finished second on the stage, which gave me a lot of confidence for the rest of the race. I was the best climber in the group that day, so I had a real advantage.

Then I finished third in the time trial, which I was really happy about, considering how I didn't have a special time trial bike. And as you may well know, when it comes to time trialing, aerodynamics is everything. I might not have won the stage, but I did cut my losses and manage to hold on to the lead. At the end of the week, I became one of the only riders in the history of the Peace Race to win it without earning a stage victory.

But I won, and for an old East German like me, it was like winning the Tour de France. Of course, I never came close to winning the Tour de France, but even to this day, the Peace Race remains one of my most memorable victories.

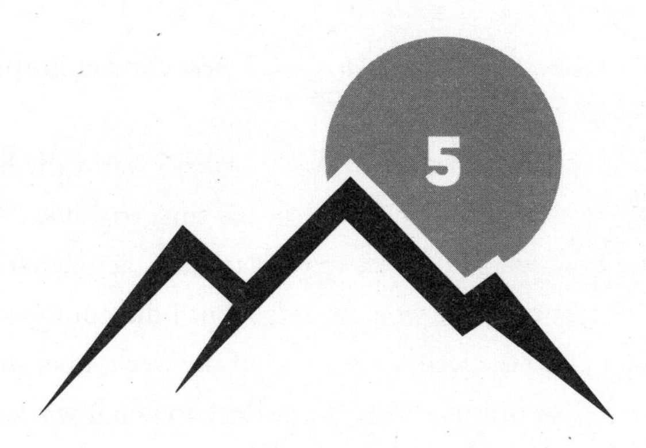

FIRST PROFESSIONAL CONTRACT

"Nope, we can't let you enter. There's a race going on!"

Jens as seen by Samuel Abt, who wrote about bicycle racing for more than 30 years for the *International Herald Tribune* and the *New York Times*:

The first of many times I interviewed Jens Voigt was during the 1999 Tour de France, and I was struck immediately by his upbeat manner and his way of brushing aside disappointments in the race. When he told me how he came to be riding for Crédit Agricole, I realized that he had overcome many setbacks before.

Despite a strong record as a member of Germany's national amateur team, he found it nearly impossible to find a job when he decided to turn professional in 1997.

"I made a little book about me, what races I did and the years, how many kilometers I trained, and I sent it to the top 22 teams," he said. "I really put a big effort into it: colors and photographs and printed on a computer; really nice. Then I had it translated into English and French.

"I sent it to the teams and I said: 'Hey, please at least answer me. Say yes or no, but answer me. What's the story?' But only two teams answered, Festina and Rabobank, and both said no."

The Telekom team in his native Germany was especially uninterested. "I tried for three years to get a contract with them, and they never wanted me," Voigt said.

He finally signed with the ZVVZ-Giant team in Australia, performed well, and was recommended by officials there to Crédit Agricole, then under the colors of the GAN insurance company. In his first season in France in 1998, he rode so well that he was elected third-leading racer of the year in Germany, behind Erik Zabel and Jan Ullrich of Telekom.

"I think Telekom would like to have me now," Voigt said with a laugh. "Too late. I'm happy where I am."

It was a pretty story, and I wrote it at the end of an account of that day's stage. Considering his pluck then, I'm not surprised that, over the long years ahead, Jens Voigt would move up in my reporting from the bottom of an article to the top.

IN 1994, I WAS AT THE HEIGHT OF MY AMATEUR CAREER. I'd won the overall World Cup competition after winning the Peace Race, not to mention the Commonwealth Bank Classic in Australia. But still I could not get a professional contract.

At the time, Germany really only had one professional team, Team Telekom, and they just weren't interested in me. I mean, every time we would race together in some mixed pro-am race, I would ask them, "So is there a chance for me to ride with you?" But it just didn't happen. For two full years, this went on, and by 1996, I was basically on my knees pleading with them, saying "I'm a good rider. Just give me a chance!"

But Walter Godefroot, the general manager, was unmoved. And to this day, I don't know why the doors of Team Telekom remained closed to me. Was it something I said? Did somebody speak badly about me behind my back? I just don't know.

You know, though, sometimes I have to thank Telekom for not taking me. Often, I think that one of the reasons I've had such a long career is that I struggled for so long to get my first professional contract. I knew how hard I'd worked to finally get a shot at the pro ranks, and so I just never, ever took it for granted!

By the end of 1996, some small German teams were coming up, but finally I had an offer from an up-and-coming Australian team. With backing from the Czech Republic, and a onetime East German coach in Heiko Salzwedel, the little ZVVZ-Giant team was the first to give me an opportunity to race professionally. Heiko had largely been responsible for the rise of track cycling in Australia after working with the AIS, the Australian Institute of Sport.

At first, I was set to go with a new team run by Hans-Michael Holczer, who would later run the Gerolsteiner professional team. I had given him my okay just before leaving for Australia to race in the Commonwealth Bank Classic at the end of 1996. But that opportunity fell through at the last minute.

I remember it well, because I had just arrived in Australia in October, and another German rider from the Nuremberg team said, "Hey, Jens, did you hear? Holczer's team isn't going to happen."

I said, "What? This is not possible!" Now again, this was before the Internet and portable telephones were commonplace. So there I was, halfway around the world, hearing that my first professional contract had just fallen through.

To make matters worse, I had just refused a contract with Heiko's ZVVZ-Giant team. At first, I had a lead with Nuremberg, but I didn't like the way they nickeled-and-dimed me simply because they thought I was desperate to sign.

So I went back to Heiko and said, "Heiko, I know I said no to you just a couple of weeks ago, but here's the situation. And if you still have a place for me, I would like to ride for you."

He said, "Okay, give me a couple of days and let me see." And a couple of days later, he came back to me and said, "Okay, we have a place." I was actually being paid by the Czech sponsor, but I was riding with young Australians such as Matthew White and a guy whom I would later meet up with again in France, Jay Sweet.

Things started out well. My first race was the Tour of Malaysia, where I finished second overall. I made tons of money at that race and was feeling pretty good about turning professional, but then we came back to Europe and just got our heads kicked in!

I'll never forget my first race in France, the Grand Prix Cholet-Pays de Loire. I got dropped with a small group, and by the time I hit the finishing circuit, the road was closed. The race official just said, "Nope, we can't let you enter. There's a race going on!"

We had just come from racing in the heat and were not ready for the low temperatures and the high speeds. That was a proper, seriously hard race. Then we went to the Critérium International and things continued to go poorly, so poorly, in fact, that I was the only survivor. Can you imagine? I was the only rider on my team to finish a two-day race! Of course, the Critérium would prove to be one of my best races, and I would win it five times. But not this year!

About the only positive note in the Critérium that year was that I started the final time trial between two established stars, Evgeni Berzin and Tony Rominger. They were both on big teams, and there I was, a neo-pro with ZVVZ-Giant, and I didn't even have a time trial bike. But I was quite proud of the fact that even on my road bike, no one was able to catch me. That in itself was a small victory.

Worse than the racing, though, was that about halfway through the season, our Czech sponsor, ZVVZ, announced that they would not be able to continue supporting the team the following year. They produced a lot of air conditioners, and a large part of their customer base was in the Middle East. The problem was that with all the tensions with Iraq and Iran, especially after the first Iraq War, NATO suddenly forbade them to sell air conditioners in these countries because they feared that some of the parts of their air conditioners could apparently be used by Iraq to cool down its nuclear weapons facilities. So, suddenly, ZVVZ lost a huge part of their market and had to make huge layoffs. As a result, sponsoring a professional cycling team was no longer justifiable.

Soon enough, it was back to the drawing board. I was looking once again for a professional contract, and I wasn't getting anywhere. Fortunately, Roger Legeay showed interest with the French GAN team. Heiko had been trying to find a place for me and actually had contacted Denis Roux, a retired pro who had ridden for Roger's team and was now a coach on the team. At first, there was some skepticism. I guess you could say that I was already a victim of my own success, because the directors on the big teams were like, "Hey, if this Jens guy has so many points, why haven't we heard of him? There must be some problem."

But Roger gave me a chance. He sent me a plane ticket and flew me to Paris, where the team picked me up. I met up with Roger the night before the Paris-Tours race, and we sat down and talked. It was basically an interview, because he wanted to know more about me, where I came from, what I thought I could do for the team, what I thought my place in cycling would be. I guess I passed the interview, because soon enough, I signed a contract.

While I had some of my fondest memories with the GAN team, I cannot say the same about this postcard where I am looking pale and overweight. (Courtesy of Jens Voigt)

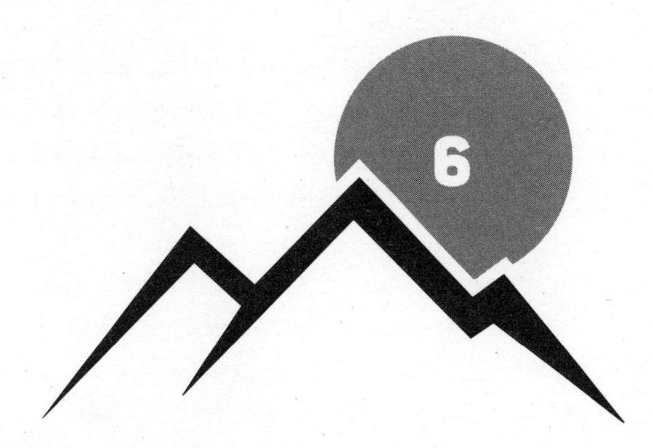

CYCLING'S BIG TIME

"What is a wheel called? *Une roue*?"

Jens as seen by Roger Legeay (former manager of the Peugeot, Z, GAN, and Crédit Agricole teams):

As every team manager does toward the end of the season, I was looking around for a few good riders to fill out our squad in the autumn of 1997. Suddenly, I came across the CV of a rider I'd never heard of: Jens Voigt. And when I looked him up, I noticed that he was already one of the top-50 ranked riders in the world. I was dumbfounded! How does some unknown guy get into the top 50? Obviously, because he was on a small team, he didn't get into the big races that carry a lot of points. So that means he really had to have a lot of results in the races he did do. It was impressive. He'd already won the Peace Race, one of the world's best amateur races. Normally, winning such a race would be a passport, a sort of guarantee, for a big contract. But for whatever reason, Jens didn't manage to find another team.

So I contacted him and met him. I liked what I saw and hired him. It's safe to say that he had a look all his own. And, at first, the guys on the team didn't know what to make of him. But he had already had a lot of good results, and that's what mattered to me.

Today Jens remains one of the recruits I'm most proud of, because I honestly think that if I hadn't given him his chance with Team GAN, Jens Voigt would have been one of those promising riders that never broke into cycling's big time. He was already 25 or 26 years old. That's late to sign with a big pro team, so it would have been difficult for him to find another team. And what a loss that would have been!

He proved himself immediately, and what a career! And Jens didn't forget the opportunity he had in coming to GAN. A couple of years later when he really had a lot of good results, Team Telekom, the big German team at the time, tried to hire him. Obviously, they had missed a huge German rider when they failed to sign him earlier, and they had the money to bring him back. But Jens never forgot. He said, "No, no, I'm with Roger, and I'm staying with Roger."

It would have been logical for him to return to Germany, but he never questioned his place on my team. It was pure Jens. From the beginning, he forged his own path. And that's what makes him so unique. If he had been on a German team, he would have been just another German on a German team. His career was so remarkable, in part, because he was so, well, international.

I FINALLY SIGNED MY FIRST BIG PRO CONTRACT WITH TEAM GAN AT THE END OF 1997. God, I remember it well! It was the night before the Paris-Tours race in October. I showed up with my "hockey player" haircut. You know, short in the front, long in the back. A mullet, essentially. At least that's what people tell me. I guess I already stood out. My soon-to-be teammates were like, "Where in the hell did Roger find this guy? Where does Roger find these people?" But Roger Legeay, the team manager, wasn't affected by such things. You know, Roger had been recruiting foreign riders for years on teams such as Peugeot, Z, and GAN and had already worked with American cycling legend Greg LeMond as well as my new teammates, such as British rider Chris Boardman and Australian Stuart O'Grady. None of those guys came from countries with a big cycling tradition, but they were all exceptional athletes. So by the time I showed up with my best "Wayne

Gretzky" haircut, Roger had enough experience in the sport to know that you can't judge a book by its cover! And he gave me a chance. It was the only chance I really needed.

I remember I earned 11,000 francs a month. Today that would only be about 1,700 euros, basically nothing by professional standards. But I didn't care! I remember getting an offer from a small German team as well, for about 95,000 deutsche marks a year, almost three times as much, but I really wanted to ride for a major team, and Roger gave me that chance.

Stephanie, my wife, was there for me, too, and really helped at this critical moment. We already had one kid, our first son, Marc. I had to choose between an easy life riding for a well-paying team located just an hour-and-a-half from Berlin or to ride for this French team for a lot less money. I could stay in Germany, race easier races, and win easier races. But no! I decided to throw it out the window for a shit contract in a foreign country! Stephanie was really cool with that, just really supportive. She was like, "If it's important for you, go for it!"

And there were real consequences. We had to give up our apartment in Berlin. She had to move back in with her parents with our first son. And I went off to France. It must sound stupid in retrospect. I only had a one-year contract. I only had one chance. But I didn't want to give up that one chance to really make it. At least that way I could always say I gave it my best shot. Even if it didn't work out, when I got old, I would never say to myself that I didn't give it a shot. There would be no "ifs." And there would be no "what-ifs."

You know, I've met a lot of good riders who didn't take their chances to go pro so that they could compete in the Olympics or something. And those people almost always regretted it. I knew one rider who had a tryout as a *stagiaire* with PDM. He has pictures of himself with Sean Kelly and Greg LeMond. But he stayed amateur so he could compete in the Olympics the next year. In the end, he never turned professional, and he's regretted it ever since!

And I know myself. I would be mad at myself if I had chosen to ride for that small German team. I would be miserable with myself. And I would be mad and miserable with myself until the end of my life! The money is a nice by-product. It's a nice bonus. But what really counts is proving to yourself that you have what it takes. At least that was what mattered to me. I just wanted to prove that I was alive and part of this sport at its highest level!

So I signed with Roger and the GAN team to ride with them in 1998. I didn't know one word of French except "*Voulez-vous coucher avec moi*?" And I didn't even know what that meant! I remember some of the boys on my team would ask me if I spoke any French, and I would just say, "Yeah, *voulez-vous coucher avec moi*?" And they would just sort of look at me! I don't know if I said it to Roger, though. That might have been a bit much!

I do remember one thing, however. I didn't have much time to prepare for this new life. I did a crash course in French just before going to the first training camp in January. The classes were held close to my house in Berlin. I'll never forget the first day of class. I came back and Stephanie asked, "So how did it go?" And I was like, "Great, my teacher is this young woman named Emmanuelle!" Now this was around the time that all those erotic *Emmanuelle* movies were making their way around the world, and you should have seen Stephanie's face. It was priceless! She just said, "What, are you kidding me?" And I was like, "No, no, she's a short, married brunette and wears glasses!"

But soon enough my little prep class in French was over. As I said, it was a crash course. And then I was off. I stuffed all my things into my car, an Opel Astra. I must have looked pretty funny driving this little Astra down the autobahn with three bikes on the roof, including my mountain bike, a race bike, and a training bike with fenders. I had everything I needed for the winter. But inside the car, it was even worse. There was my television, my microwave, silverware, cups, plates, just everything. My whole life was in that car!

But from the get-go, everything was perfectly organized by Roger

Legeay and his logistics manager, Michel Laurent. Now this was back in the day before the Internet exploded. Everything arrived in the mail, every plane ticket, paychecks, everything. And in my six years with the team, they never missed a click. I never missed one flight, and even with all the French holidays and everything, my paychecks always arrived on time. And every year, in December, a big box arrived with everything I needed to start out the new season. It contained all my new team clothes, the team backpack, the new team bike, just everything I needed. And never once was there the slightest hiccup, never one missed payment, nothing. Unbelievable, just unbelievable!

But that doesn't mean things were easy. Even after my little crash course with Emmanuelle, my French was, how do you say, *basique*? I remember taking out a piece of paper and drawing a bike and asking my teammates, "What is a wheel called? *Une roue*? What is a tire called? What is a derailleur called?" Then I took out another piece of paper and drew a body and asked, "What is an arm called? What is a leg called? What is a hand called?" Then I sketched all a cyclist's clothes on the body and said, "What are leg warmers called? What is a jersey called? What are shoes called?" And that's how I learned French! Pretty basic, huh?

Training with my buddies around the hills of Toulouse in 1999. I only have good memories of the six years I lived and trained there. (James Startt)

MOVING TO FRANCE

"Oh my God! They're going to fire me!"

Jens as seen by Chris Boardman (former hour record holder and teammate to Voigt on GAN and Crédit Agricole):

Jens, quite simply, extended my career by two full years. By 1998, when he came on board with the GAN team, I was having a tough time. It was getting harder and harder to win anything. But when Jens came into the team, everything for him was an adventure, everything! It was brilliant. He was brilliant! He just chose this attitude at the start of his life that said pretty much, "I'm going to look for ways to have an adventure." That's exactly what he did, looked at everything as an adventure.

And it was contagious! It could be cold and raining, and he would say, "Oh my God, man! I'm just going to smash it!" And he would do just that! Or he could just be watching some stupid cartoon about a cow and a chicken in the hotel bedroom and you would get this hilarious running commentary while you were taking a shower. I remember he didn't really ever go to sleep. He just became unconscious. There was this sudden shift in being, one from being this sort of manic child to just being dead to the world!

And then he would wake up in the morning fully recharged. He was just amazing!

We roomed together a lot. I think somebody thought he would be good for me. And they were right!

BARELY AFTER ARRIVING IN FRANCE, I WAS OFF TO MY FIRST TRAINING CAMP WITH THE GAN TEAM. And things didn't go all that smoothly, at least not that first day, that first ride. We were off somewhere in the north of France, like in Normandy, at a place called the Center Parc. This was before the days when training camps were always held in Spain or someplace warm, and my first memory is of the cold.

But what I remember more than the weather was that first ride with the team. To this day, I wish I could redo that ride. There were 17 of us, not 18, riding two abreast. And as one of the new pros, I was the odd man out, the one guy riding alone in the pace line. And I'm riding in the middle of the pack, when all of a sudden, this big truck comes by with a sailboat on it. And I like boats, especially sailboats. They just look BEAUTIFUL! Just looking at them gives me some peace of mind. And so there it was, this huge, long truck with a sailboat on it. I thought, "Wow!" I just looked back and watched it go by. And boy, was that the wrong thing to do! That was it! I just watched the boat, looked back, touched a wheel in front of me, and crashed. I crashed on my first training camp! Heck, I crashed on my first training ride with my new team!

I was so embarrassed! I was like, "Oh my God! They're going to fire me! Oh my God!"

But everyone was so supportive. They all stopped and came back. Guys kept saying, "Are you okay? Are you okay?" And I just jumped up and said, "Ah yeah, yeah, it's nothing! Of course I'm okay. Just a little blood on my knee, that's all!" I felt terrible, just terrible! I'd crashed on my first day. Chris Boardman was there. Chris was a huge champion, but he was also very British and had that oh-so-British humor. And he was just standing there saying, "Ah, that's it. You just failed the test! End of contract!" It was all in good humor, but Chris was my team leader. So that was how my first day of training went. A truly auspicious beginning, no?

I remember at that first training camp, they put me in the same room with Chris, probably because he spoke good English. And, actually, we became very close. But down in the main hall, I would sit down with my French teammates, such as Anthony Langella and Sébastien Hinault. And in the evenings, I would get out my notebook and show them my drawings. I would point to a body part on my little stick-figure drawing and ask them how to say it in French. They laughed a lot at me, but I think they appreciated the effort I was making. At least that's what I kept telling myself!

Then, directly after the training camp, I moved straight to Toulouse, where a lot of my teammates were living. On that little itty-bitty salary, I couldn't even think about getting an apartment on my own, but that's when I learned just how cool and open the Australians could be, because Stuart O'Grady and Henk Vogels just took me in like I was one of their own. Jay Sweet was there, too, although he was riding for the Aubervilliers team. So I just moved in with the boys for the first month.

Roger Legeay had been very direct and really wanted me to move to France. He said, "Look, you have a one-year contract. You're not a young kid anymore. I would like you to move closer to the team. We'll have a better idea of what you're up to, and you'll get better connected to our team."

I just said, "Yeah, okay then." That's all it took to cram my entire life into that little Opel. But then one of my French teammates at the time, Frédéric Moncassin, just said, "Yeah, well come live with us down in Toulouse."

Fred was the star sprinter on the team, and he really saved me down there, because getting started in France wasn't easy. To be able to rent an apartment, you need to have a French bank account. But to have a bank account, you need an address. And for both of those, you need to have pay slips for the last three months. Since I had just arrived in France, that was impossible, but Fred would come with us—me and a couple of other new riders—when we were looking for an apartment and say, "Look, I can vouch for these guys. They might not have all their pay slips just yet, but they're just neo-pros. They're going to be good." So finally I was able to get an apartment with Jay Sweet and Marcel Gono in a little village about 20 kilometers south of Toulouse.

But while the GAN team was incredibly well organized, life with the Australians was often quite the opposite. Actually, in my case, my first year with a big pro team represented a double culture shock. Not only was I training and racing in France, but I was living with a bunch of Australians. And let me tell you, that took some getting used to all on its own! I have such great memories of those early days, but hmm, how shall I say, it wasn't always ideal for getting the rest and relaxation needed to be at my best.

I'll never forget the night I returned after my first professional win. I finally made it back to Toulouse after a very long, cold day in the rain. I was happy to see the boys, but I was also really tired. Everyone was stoked when I came through the door, and I was hungry, so I said, "Hey, boys! It's the first victory for the house. Come on, I'll take you out to dinner!" All was fine and dandy, but once we were at dinner, the boys were like, "Hey, it's still the weekend. How about we just go to a little nightclub after?"

I said, "Oh, okay boys, but let's go in two cars, because I'm tired, and if you want to stay out very late, I might go home. I'll go for a little while, but I can't dance until 6:00 a.m."

As soon as we arrived at the club, we ordered a bottle of whiskey and some cola. By about midnight, I was fading pretty badly, so I said, "Okay, boys, I'm heading home!"

But as I got up to leave, I saw them raise their hands to order another bottle, and oh boy, that was just the start of it.

The next morning, I woke up and didn't see their car. Naively, at first I wondered, "Hmm, I wonder where the boys are? Maybe they got a hotel room or something." But soon enough, I saw that this was not the case. I heard noises in their rooms, and as soon as I looked at them, I knew it was going to be a whole other story. And I knew immediately that it wasn't good! So I said, "Please, boys, tell me it's not what I think it is!"

One had a black eye. One had terrible whiplash. And they were like, "Ah, ah, we don't know where the car is!" And I just said, "What? Did you have an accident?" And they were like, "Ah, ah, we think soo. . . "

Now I was not in the best shape myself. I had raced the day before and had a very long day. I guess you could say I was a little exasperated. And I said, "Are you kidding me? Come on, let's go find the car!"

And there it was, about 500 meters from the club, sitting on the median strip in the middle of a four-lane road. The car was just sitting in the grass, totaled. Honestly, I don't even know how they got out of it alive!

Trying to keep my composure, I remember saying, "Ah, hey boys, how did you make it home?"

They explained to me how they just walked back to the nightclub and called a taxi to take them home.

But then I started to think about the reality of the situation, and I said, "Boys, are you kidding me? You both have a three-month tourist visa in this country and it's now April. Think about it! That's one, two, three, four months! You two are officially ILLEGAL ALIENS! And to make matters worse, you were driving a car with outdated license plates. So you're two illegal aliens driving an illegal car drunk, leaving the scene of an accident. Are you kidding me? Are you kidding me? You guys are in SO MUCH TROUBLE!"

Finally we got a towing company to come tow the car. They obviously knew our situation, and we knew that they knew our situation. When we came back the following Monday, they just said, "Look, guys, the car is totaled. You can take the CD player, if you want, and we'll keep the car for spare parts to cover the towing." And considering that maybe only one door was still intact, I considered it a fair deal. It was really a close call, but just sort of a typical experience with the boys down in "Sydney-sur-Garonne"!

But they were great guys, and they could really suffer on a bike. I mean, Jay was the kind of rider who could just turn himself inside out on a bike when he had to.

Anyway, that was my initiation into my new Australian life in France. It was not the easiest way to move to a new country, but for the next six years, I always had a house or an apartment around Toulouse. The first year, I shared the apartment with Jay and Marcel, and then, when I got a better contract, I was able to get a place of my own and bring my wife and son down. After two years, Stephanie decided to go back to Berlin. But still I kept a place in Toulouse while I was at GAN and later Crédit Agricole. It was really and truly my home away from home!

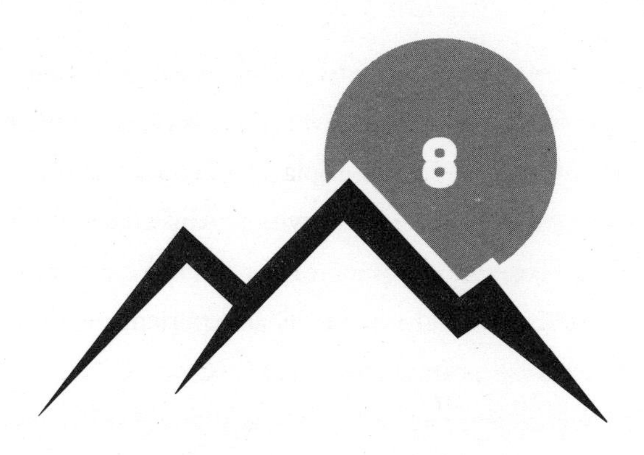

FIRST WIN

"I'm not just a pretty face!"

MY FIRST YEAR OF RACING IN THE BIG LEAGUES WAS NOT EASY. This was the start of the 1998 season, and teams such as Festina were just heroes. But that was before the Festina affair broke and we realized how doped up they were. Racing was just full gas at that time, and trying to race on that level was no easy jump for me.

But somehow I managed to get into a breakaway in my first race of the season, the Grand Prix la Marseillaise, with none other than Richard Virenque, the popular French rider and leader of Festina. I remember I accelerated going over this climb about 50 kilometers from the finish, and I actually dropped Virenque! Can you believe that? I actually dropped Richard Virenque in my first race of the year! I got over the top with another rider, Fabrice Gougot, and we waited on the top because it was too far to go to the finish. But I still ended up getting fourth that day, a decent start.

Almost as important, though, was that I was pretty much the only finisher on my team, and suddenly guys were like, "Oh wow, the neo-pro with the bad haircut is actually pretty good!" Then we went straight to the Étoile des Bessèges, the first stage race of the year in France. And I finished eighth overall, which was a huge relief for me, because I was stressing about having only a one-year contract.

Looking back on it now, knowing I had only one year probably helped me. It made me train really hard in the winter in an effort to prove myself, to find my place on the team and in the pecking order and all. I came ready to perform at the first race of the season.

But my big break came a couple of months later when I got my first professional victory, and, as it turned out, the first win for the team of the season, at the Vuelta Ciclista al País Vasco, the "Tour of the Basque country" in Spain. I'll never forget that day, and it's a race I can truly say that I have loved ever since!

How I came up with that win is another story, though. Oh man! The whole week I was just SUFFERING! The racing was so hard! They were just going so fast! And again, this was all before the Festina affair exploded. The whole week I was just like, "Oh my God! I'm a worthless-piece-of-shit rider here!" I was getting dropped all the time, and by the last day, I was about an hour-and-a-half down. But then, the night before the last stage, I remember looking at the result sheets and seeing that only three guys from our team were left in the race, François Simon, Cédric Vasseur, and me. They'd already sent the team bus back home. The next day started with a short stage before the afternoon time trial. And I remember saying to the boys before the start, "I just go! I just go! It's a short stage, and I'm so far down. I'm attacking!"

It's a standard late-race situation, where guys who are far down in the standings can attack, because the leaders don't care if you get away and win a stage at that point. But you still have to be there. You have to make that breakaway. And I remember at the start that morning, it was raining and cold once again. And I was pretty much the only one in the whole peloton who didn't have a rain jacket on. It was so obvious that I wanted to go, that I was going to attack! I had a thermal jacket but no rain jacket. Everyone else was there with long-sleeve rain jackets. As we rolled out toward the official start, I remember saying to myself, "Oh! I hope the neutral start doesn't last too long, because everyone is going to see that I don't have a rain jacket on. Everybody is going to realize that I want to attack! And as soon as we hit kilometer zero, I was just like, BANG!"

After a kilometer or two, I went full gas and then looked back. There was only Jörg Jaksche on my wheel and Paul van Hyfte a little further back, yelling "Wait, wait!" So we waited for him and then started rolling.

Laurent Jalabert and the ONCE team were leading the race, and as soon as they realized that the best guy in the breakaway was more than 15 minutes down, they gave us something like a six-minute lead, which is a lot for a 95-kilometer stage, so we clearly had a chance to stay away. Then there was a climb with about 20 kilometers to go, and I just attacked! And I managed to win the stage alone with more than a one-minute gap.

It was just amazing! For one, this is the Basque country in northern Spain, where they're just crazy about cycling. Even in the rain, they all showed up. It was packed! On the climb, everybody was in your face yelling "Venga, venga!" And Eurosport was broadcasting the race, so the whole time I was in the break, I knew my parents were watching back home in Germany. And I knew that they were on the edge of their seats! Talk about motivation!

At one point when I was off, my team director, Serge Beucherie, came up alongside me and rolled down the window. He looked over at me and nodded and just said, "*Impressionnant.*" And I was like, "Yeah, I've got a plan here!"

Now like I said, up until then, the team had had a shit race. At one point, though, Serge had to come up to me and pour hot tea over my fingers because I couldn't shift my gears anymore. What a way to get your first professional win! And the Vuelta Ciclista al País Vasco is definitely a good place to start winning, because outside the grand tours such as the Tour de France, it's considered one of the hardest races in the world. There's always a good field, and everyone who can climb even a little bit is in the Basque country that week!

I might not have been one of the best riders in that race that year, but I was just waterproof! And one thing I learned early on in my racing career was that when it rains, 50 percent of the peloton has lost the race, because, well, they have lost motivation. And since I'm already better than 50 percent of the peloton, by pure logic, I'm already top 10! You know what I like to say sometimes? "Everything that's sticky is good for me! Everything that makes you uncomfortable, whether it's rain, mud, or snow, is good for me!"

It's not that I like all that stuff, mind you! No, actually it's quite the contrary. I would love to be a sprinter, you know. I would love to be one of those guys who can just sit in the pack all day long adjusting the gel in his hair! It must be nice to simply sit in all day and then blow by everyone in the last 20 meters and get the win, get the podium, get the podium girls. Everybody loves you! That's great! I would love to do that. I would even prefer that. But I can't. It's not given to me. I've got to do it the other way, the hard way.

As you may know, I'm not just a pretty face! But for my entire career, everybody kept making the same mistake with me every time I attacked early. They'd say, "Oh, that's Jensie going in another early attack. Let him go! We'll catch him later." But they rarely did.

And sometimes, to be honest, I couldn't believe it. I'd be like, "Are you kidding me? Are you going to let me do this to you again?"

Now this was never more true than in the Critérium International race that I won five times. For three years in a row, at the very same spot, almost the same meter exactly, I would attack. And guys would come with me in the break and actually work with me. I couldn't believe it. I mean, how could they work with me? It was like the rabbit working with the fox until he gets eaten! The rabbit should run away. He should know he is going to get eaten. But for several years, the Critérium International was just like Christmas, my birthday, and my wedding day all wrapped into one! I'd be in a breakaway again, and I just knew I was going to win. All those people working so nicely with me, just waiting to get dropped by me again. Even the newspapers wrote about the exact spot I would attack. But it always worked! I couldn't believe my luck!

I remember one year, 2007 I think, I was up the road, and Alejandro Valverde had his whole team chasing me, but then he looked around and saw my teammate Frank Schleck on his wheel and said, "This is déjà vu! Jens is up the road. We're chasing like mad. But we're not getting any closer. And Jens is going to win again!" Frankie just smiled!

Getting ready to start another stage in the Pyrenees in the 1998 Tour de France. (Courtesy of Jens Voigt)

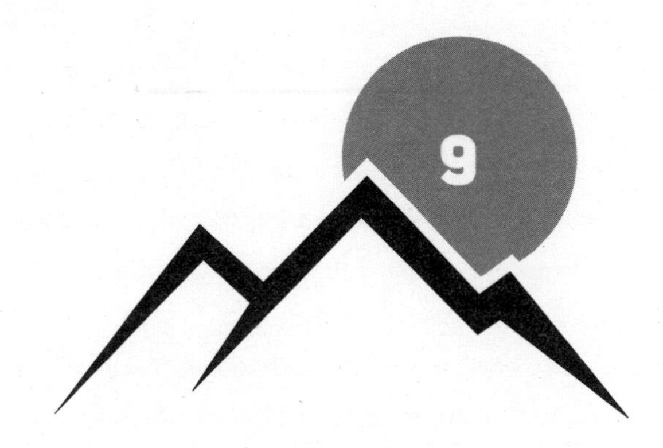

FIRST TOUR DE FRANCE

"Is this what I signed up for?"

WHEN YOU RACE FOR A FRENCH TEAM, THERE'S ONLY ONE RACE THAT COUNTS—THE TOUR DE FRANCE. And from my first days on Team GAN, everything we did pointed to the Tour. And for just about every guy on that team, the primary goal was to make the Tour de France team. I was no exception, as I had been dreaming about the Tour for years!

For me, the Tour de France just always held a sort of mystique. I remember my dad, Egon, telling me when I was growing up, "You know in the West they have another race as big as the Peace Race. They call it the Tour de France." I was only 11 or 12, just getting into the sport, but I was already hooked. Of course, East German television would not cover the Tour, but I remember the newspapers would occasionally publish the top-five results of the Tour and then, since we lived by the border, we occasionally saw bits and pieces on West German television. This was back in the day when Bernard Hinault was winning. I had no idea how to pronounce the strange mix of vowels and consonants that made up his name. I remember thinking Hinault sounded something like "Heenawult"! That must have been in 1982, when he was winning everything. I remember thinking, "Hey, that guy must be pretty good!"

But it wasn't until 1987, when the Tour actually started in Berlin, that I had my first idea of just how big the Tour de France was. Now the Berlin Wall was still very much in place at the time, so going to see the Tour was not a possibility. But I was already in sports school in Berlin, so it was easier to get Western television as well as West Berlin radio stations that were really talking up the Tour. I'll never forget watching the start of the race from my little television in my dorm room, with my little antenna pointed toward West Berlin. I was just captivated. All those colorful jerseys with all sorts of different sponsors were just so beautiful, so rich, compared to my solid gray East German national jersey! In addition to that, the prologue was won by a Polish rider, Lech Piasecki. That was such a watershed moment for me. I remember thinking, wow, if a guy like that can come from a Communist country and ride the Tour de France, maybe I can, too, someday! And from that day on, the Tour de France was my dream.

Now I think that Roger Legeay had an idea of who would make the Tour team a couple of months before. A couple of riders like our leader, Chris Boardman, our sprinter, Frédéric Moncassin, or experienced guys like Stuart O'Grady—guys that were proven—knew they were going to the Tour. But that wasn't the case for a lot of us. Like I said, all the French riders wanted to go to the Tour, so there were a lot of guys competing for few places.

In hindsight, I think Roger knew for a couple of months that he wanted to put me in the Tour, but there were so many guys campaigning to be on the team, and I was just the young neo-pro! As a result, I really didn't know until the last minute.

But I'd won my first race already at the Vuelta Ciclista al País Vasco, the first team victory of the season. And then I had a good race in the Critérium du Dauphiné-Libéré, a key warm-up race for the Tour. My teammate, Chris Boardman, won the prologue, and I got in a break with Maximilian Sciandri on Stage 1. My team director just told me to take my pulls and see where things would go, and soon enough, we had a big gap. By the finish, we had more than three minutes on the peloton, and I was wearing the yellow jersey. I was just like, "How cool is this?!" Clearly my opportunistic approach to racing was starting to pay off, even if I wasn't anywhere near the strongest guy in the race. I was already figuring out how to find opportunities for myself. I lost the lead a couple of days later when we climbed up the Mont Ventoux, but I showed that even if I wasn't in the same league as the great champions, I was okay. I could hold my own. And that was important for my confidence heading into the Tour. Soon enough, I had my ticket for Dublin, Ireland, where the Tour would start.

Everything was like a dream. We spent a lot of time preparing for the prologue start around the streets of Dublin, and I was really trying to learn everything I could from Chris Boardman, who was just about the best time trialer in the world at that moment.

And we were, of course, ecstatic when Chris won the race, because winning the prologue takes so much pressure off the team, it's not even funny. It was so good to have the jersey!

You know, it's one thing to say that the Tour de France is the world's biggest bike race, the greatest, whatever, but it's another thing to see it from the inside. For one, at the start, you get a completely new bike, a new set of clothes, a new helmet, new glasses, new shoes. You start out fresh. Every day you see all the cars and buses being washed down. And the riders are the same. Everyone has just had a fresh haircut. Everyone is freshly shaved. Everyone is fit and skinny. Everyone is in his prime.

You see the way people behave, the attention to everything, and the attention to us! Suddenly there are all these interview requests after nobody gave a damn about you for the first half of the year!

Generally, as in Dublin that year, the race starts with a prologue. And when you go out and do the reconnaissance of the course, there are already signs on the roads. There are already spectators. Already the speed, just in training, is so much higher because everybody is so fit. You sense immediately that it's a much bigger game.

I'll never forget that first Tour with Chris. You could just tell he was more focused. He talked less. He spent hours outside with the mechanics checking his bike, checking his position, discussing the best tire pressure. You could see the intensity rising.

But all this time the biggest scandal in the history of the Tour to date was brewing—the Festina affair.

While in Ireland, we were getting news and hearing rumors that one of the Festina assistants, one of the *soigneurs*, or physical therapists, had been stopped and that drugs were found in the car. We were hearing that there was a problem with Festina. But we didn't know what was going on exactly. Now, you have to remember that this was before the Internet had really taken off, and it was before everyone had mobile phones. Information traveled a lot more slowly back then.

So it wasn't until the Tour returned to France that we (the riders) understood the full scope of the Festina affair. Within a day or so, everything really blew up. We already started hearing that Festina would be excluded from the race. And the more the press wrote about it, the more we understood that we were living through the biggest scandal ever in our sport so far.

And for me as a neo-pro, I was just shocked at how organized the doping had become on that team. Everybody on my team was shocked. Was everybody on that team involved in the doping program one way or another? Did everybody do it? Did everybody know? Was everybody a part of it?

At first, in our innocent little ways, we thought that maybe the doping was just isolated to them. You have to remember that Festina, at the time, was one of the biggest teams with one of the biggest budgets. But as the race went on, we understood that Festina was not alone.

Throughout that first week or so, it seemed that not a day went by without more bad news. Police were checking cars and trucks at borders and at gas stations. Not a day went by without another rider being caught, another suitcase being found with drugs. It just didn't stop! We were like, "Are you kidding? This is ridiculous!" The Dutch TVM team was searched, and members of the team were taken to the police station, where they spent much of the night, before being released without charges. And teams, especially the Spanish teams, just stopped racing. They quit and went home!

Italian racer Rodolfo Massi, who took over the best-climber jersey from me in the Pyrénées, got kicked out of the race. Then we had a riders' strike, where we were all sitting on the road. And it was just like, "Ah man, could somebody please translate for me? When is this going to stop?" Nobody knew if the Tour was going to continue. Nobody knew if the racing would actually make it to the finish line in Paris. It was that bad!

There I am in my first Tour de France, sitting on the road in the middle of a rider protest. And at one point, I just asked myself, "Is this what I signed up for? This is what I get for working so hard to become a professional?" Ever since the Berlin Wall came down, I'd had only one dream—to be a professional and ride in the Tour de France. Suddenly I just thought, "And that's all it is?" My dream was disintegrating before my eyes. Everything was shattering before my eyes!

Even my parents called and said, "Son, what's going on over there?"

And all I could say was, "I don't know much more than you do!" Again, there was no Internet to speak of. Information was just traveling a lot slower.

And it continued and continued every day for the entire three weeks. Every day someone from the German press would come up to me with a question regarding some information they had heard, some source. I was so confused. I didn't know what I was supposed to say. I didn't possess any inside knowledge. I was just in shock mode.

Later, as riders continued to get popped over the years, I became more vocal and switched into anger mode, saying publicly, "Haven't they learned yet? This shit is not good for our sport or for us!" But at that moment, in the middle of the 1998 Tour de France, I was too overwhelmed to even be angry.

Needless to say, we talked about it a lot around the dinner table and in our hotel rooms at night, trying to figure it all out, because let me tell you, I was not the only one who was confused. Nobody else really understood what was going on, either.

But when I think back on those days, I can tell you I was really happy to have a teammate and a team leader like Chris Boardman. Chris and I hit it off on a lot of things, and in many ways, we were on the same wavelength. Like me, Chris is a real family guy. And he was always saying, "You have to decide what you want. When all this is over, do you want to be able to go to a barbecue or go to the beach with your kids and be healthy? Do you want to go out in public and be able to hold your head up? Or do you want to read in the papers, or worse, have *your kids* read somewhere that you've been in prison? It's just not worth it!"

You know, looking back, with all the other doping problems that hit the sport afterward, it's sometimes difficult for people to recall just how devastating and how traumatic the Festina affair was for any of us who lived through it. But I can tell you that for anyone near the Tour de France at the time, the Festina affair was a real wake-up call. And for me, I can tell you that from that moment on, if anyone would have come up to me and offered me "some help," well, I would just say, "Go fuck yourself!" There was just no way in hell I would have any of that shit happen to me! Doping just isn't right. Doping is dangerous. Doping is unhealthy. Doping just destroys everything! I guess you can say that at least the Festina affair set me up for the rest of my career. It marked me forever.

I had other reminders of just how dangerous the doping circle can be and how it can destroy lives, as well.

I'll never forget several years later, in 2001, after I'd worn the yellow jersey in the Tour and had managed to have quite a few wins, my hometown in Dassow named a street after me, Jens Voigt Ring.

It was great—a real honor—but unfortunately, as you all know, the doping scandals continued well after the Festina affair. Anyway, I remember coming home, and at one point, I remember my mom and dad saying, "Listen, son, we're not there all the time with you. But if you do that shit, we would drop dead! We couldn't live here anymore. They named a street after you. We live on Number 1 Jens Voigt Ring. If you would do that and get caught, we couldn't go out on the street in daylight anymore. We'd have to move to another country! We would be so ashamed. We'd drop dead!"

Those were powerful words, and yet another reminder to me that doping doesn't just hurt you, it hurts everyone you love!

I think if you talk to people who lived through the Festina affair, many will agree that it was a sort of healing shock. And for a while at least, things seemed to get better. I wouldn't say that the racing was any slower. It just seemed more even.

Unfortunately, that period of more even racing didn't seem to last, and two or three years after Festina, it seemed like some people had returned to their old habits, had returned to their old programs.

And so the scandals continued, reminding us that not everything had changed. In 1999, Marco Pantani tested positive and couldn't defend his Tour de France title. There was the "Blitz" during the Giro d'Italia, the "Tour of Italy," in 2001. There was Tyler Hamilton in 2004 and then Operación Puerto in Spain in 2006, which implicated a number of riders. And, of course, there was always suspicion around Lance Armstrong, a suspicion that proved to be true, as we found out many years later.

Frankly, there were times when I asked myself whether cycling could even survive. I mean, just looking back over the past 10 years at the podiums in the Giro or the Vuelta is enough to make you think they're all poisonous. And the Tour de France obviously has had its dark spots, too. No, honestly, at times I wondered if the whole sport of bike racing wasn't just going to stop, and that would be the end of it. There were times when I just sat there and said, "Another one? Haven't they learned anything yet? Don't they realize it's not worth the risk? Don't they realize that doping will come back and bite them in the ass?"

For me at least, and I know for many of my teammates at the time, the 1998 Tour de France was just such a jolt. People who lived through that really didn't want to live through it again. I felt like whoever didn't hear the bell then and there was beyond help! It was so incredibly clear that the sport had to change, and change radically.

I'm sure that being on a French team at the time heightened our awareness of the gravity of the situation. I mean, this was France, home of the Tour de France, a national landmark. And the Tour had just been brought to its knees!

In the off-season that year, there was a lot of brainstorming, as a lot of people were trying to find ways to save the sport, trying to find solutions so that the sport could regain its credibility.

Our principal team sponsor, GAN, was replaced by Crédit Agricole, and from the first day of the first training camp, the message was very clear. Roger Legeay, our manager, spoke at the first get-together, and right then and there he laid out his point of view. It was quite simple. I still remember it. He said, "Dope is an absolute no-go. This is point zero. We have a clean slate, and it's up to us to write cycling history on good terms. We have seen what drugs have done to the Tour. We have seen how much damage drugs have done to the sport. We have seen how it threatens all our livelihoods. I would rather that we finish second, third, fourth, or tenth and know we did it the right way, than win and have to worry that a year later or two years later, the truth comes out that we were doping." He couldn't have been more clear.

In addition, Roger really started cutting back on the amount of outside help riders were getting and pressured us to work only with the team doctor. The reasoning was simple. If an individual rider or doctor gets into trouble, it still comes back to the team. Now that sort of thing gets really complicated in cycling, since riders are living all over the world. But Roger said clearly that if we used any other doctors, coaches, or advisers, they were obliged to file detailed paperwork with the team.

The French government got involved, as well, and started what was known as the *études longitudinales,* long-term testing that was very similar to the biological passport that the International Cycling Union put into place years later. With the études longitudinales we would get a letter in the mail every few weeks summoning us to an appointment at a certain hospital or clinic, where we would have to give urine and blood samples. These samples would be collected and tested over time to clearly illustrate any suspicious fluctuations in a rider that could be a sign of doping. If a rider's testosterone level suddenly jumped up before the Tour de France, for example, that could be a suspicious sign. The authorities also made it very clear to us that the samples would be stored over time and probably would be retested. It was definitely a way to scare people off from doing crazy things.

The police were also involved. New anti-doping laws were quickly put into place. In other countries, it took a few years before doping was considered a crime, but in France, it happened very quickly. Previously, doping in sports fell only under the jurisdiction of sporting federations, but that all changed after the Festina affair. You really have to give France credit. They were simply ahead of their time and the first to take a really strong anti-doping initiative. And I know that for the French teams at the time, teams such as Crédit Agricole, La Française des Jeux, and others, it was very clear that doping wasn't a possibility.

Personally I could feel the difference in the years that followed. In 1998 I won one race in the Vuelta Ciclista al País Vasco on what was basically a fluke. But I also spent a lot of time that year just hanging on. There were times in 1997 and 1998 where I just felt like a shit rider. I felt like I was hopeless! I felt like I was never going to be anybody. Later on, I learned why some guys were so much better.

In the years that followed, however, I won a lot more races, more consistently. In 1999, I won my first Critérium International, a much bigger race with more international riders. And, as I have mentioned, I won that race a total of five times over the years. I wasn't hanging on for dear life anymore. I just felt closer to the best. I felt that the playing field was more level.

But like I said, there were also signs that some riders were returning to their old ways, because there were still a lot of doping scandals and a lot of riders testing positive. Some performances just looked too much like those before Festina. Sometimes you would see a rider who was just shit all spring suddenly go BANG! They would make this amazing transformation from a fat little caterpillar into a beautiful butterfly, and you would have to wonder. Some guys, it seemed, would pass me without ever catching up to me.

In France, they started speaking of *cyclisme à deux vitesses,* cycling at two speeds. But I really never was a big fan of this term, because too many people used it as an excuse. French cycling at the time was also a bit stuck in the past. The sport was managed by a lot of directors who were old pros. And many of them thought that because they had trained a certain way 20 years ago, the young riders of the day should do exactly the same. For a while, they missed the shift to more modern training methods. They wouldn't pay attention to nutrition. They would still have red wine on the table. Some were like, "Wind tunnel testing! Why should I do that?" They took their time using power output systems like SRM, or even simple things like interval training, which everybody does today.

And also during this time, you had to be careful not to accuse somebody wrongly, because most often you just didn't know. The truth might come out years later about some performance, but when you're out there on the road, you don't know. That's why it was always important for me to give a rider the benefit of the doubt. And I certainly didn't want people to talk badly about me behind my back. It's easy to point fingers. If you're beaten, it's easy to become miserable or jealous. It's easy to say, "Ah, I think he's doing this or doing that!" That's easy. So I was very suspicious of this *deux vitesses* thing, even though you couldn't help but question some performances.

One thing that helped me keep my head up was that, on a personal level, I was winning races. Over the years, I have won something like 65 races with International Cycling Union points. I had a good career. It's not like I was beaten all the time. No, I had a good, long career with some good wins. I was always fortunate, too, that there was a place for my style of riding. I made my niche as a long-break rider, and there has always been room in the sport for that sort of opportunistic style of riding. There are always days when the big favorites just aren't going to chase you down. There are always days in a long stage race where groups go out and make it to the finish. So I had my chances—plenty of them—and I took them.

So for me, at least, it was easier to explain defeat. I could just say, "Okay, maybe I'm not a big stage-race rider, at least not overall. Maybe I just can't climb well enough or ride time trials fast enough because I'm simply a big guy, and I create more air resistance." And I was okay with that. Again, I won 65 races over the years. That's better than a kick in the teeth!

In what was definitely one of my all-time great moments on a bike, I celebrate the team time trial victory in the 2001 Tour de France with my Crédit Agricole teammates. (Yuzuru Sunada)

CRÉDIT AGRICOLE DAYS

"If you try to win, you might lose.
But if you don't try to win, you'll lose for sure!"

I SPENT SIX YEARS WITH ROGER LEGEAY ON THE GAN AND CRÉDIT AGRICOLE TEAMS, AND THEY WERE DEFINITELY SIX OF MY BEST YEARS AS A PROFESSIONAL. It was here where I met lifelong friends such as Stuart O'Grady, Thor Hushovd, and Bobby Julich.

Probably my best memory from those years was that of the 2001 Tour de France, which was not only a breakthrough for me, but for the entire team. On Stage 2, we decided to go on the attack, and shortly after rolling out of Calais that day, I got into an early breakaway. We were eventually caught by 12 other riders, including Stuart, as we raced into and across Belgium. And although we didn't win the stage that finished in Antwerp, it positioned Stuey perfectly to take over the yellow jersey the next day, which started a great run for the team that year.

With O'Grady in yellow after Stage 3, we controlled the race for much of the first week, and it set us up perfectly for one of our greatest rides ever: the team time trial (TTT).

Now the team time trial is a very special event, because it's really about the team. The riders all start together, and a minimum of five must finish together. No team is stronger than its weakest element, and the team with the strongest riders in the race can be beaten by a team that simply rides better together, which was very much true of our team in 2001.

For Roger Legeay, the TTT was always an essential event. He just loved it and took it very seriously. Don't forget, Roger had worked with guys like Greg LeMond and Chris Boardman. He had seen how Greg won the 1989 Tour de France by 8 seconds in the final time trial, and he saw Chris win the prologue time trial in both the 1996 and 1998 Tours de France. So he took time trialing very, very seriously.

He had seen how Greg used special aerodynamic handlebars to beat Laurent Fignon in 1989. That impressed Roger, so he was very good about getting the best equipment for us. He actually rented out the entire Le Mans 24-hour speedway for two or three days so we could do special training. Can you imagine that? Renting out this legendary automobile track just for one cycling team?

And every day, as we trained on the track, Roger would drive behind us and shout through a loudspeaker attached to the hood of the car to tell us exactly when to pull off and whom to jump in behind as we were fading back. We had certain signals to communicate, like if we needed to skip a turn and sit out for a bit.

But mostly what I remember throughout the whole 60- to 70-kilometer effort was Roger yelling various instructions to us every 20 to 30 seconds. "*Derrière Anthony Morin, Jens! Derrière Sébastien Hinault! Jens à la 6ème position*!" That really was a big help, because we didn't have to waste time thinking about stuff like how long to pull, and that way we avoided getting behind a tiring rider. So we learned how to be the most efficient we could possibly be. And that paid off big-time in the Tour de France.

And I will never forget when we won the team time trial that day in Bar-le-Duc. It was just a huge day for us, superb! And we won that race because we really were the strongest and smoothest team. But everything didn't go perfectly. The stage started in Verdun and rolled past all these World War I battlefields. All along the course, about every kilometer, we would pass a soldier dressed up in a commemorative blue WWI uniform. But it was raining the whole time, so it was very dismal. And quite dangerous. We had a puncture and had to wait for Bobby Julich. Then, when Anthony Morin also punctured, we just had to leave him. It was just like, "Sorry, Tony, go back to the second team car, get a new wheel, and do the best you can. We can't wait for you!" So it was not an easy day for us—far from it!

But despite the setbacks, we really had a good train rolling, and we beat huge teams such as US Postal, ONCE, and Team Telekom. With Stuey in yellow, we were the last team to start, which really helps in a time trial, because you always know where you are compared to your opponents; you hear their time splits ahead of you. It was one of those magical days when we were just clicking. Midway through the day, we sort of knew that if we didn't "biff" it in a corner or something, we were going to win. We were really flying. You could feel it. And we were taking time from our opponents at each time check, yet we weren't going all out! I can still remember Roger on the radio telling us, "Okay, guys, you have the fastest time splits. Don't take any risks! You don't need to speed up! You're going to win!"

At the finish, we were all hugging each other, the mechanics, the *soigneurs* or physical therapists, the riders, everyone! We just had an incredible bond on that team, and together we enjoyed one of my greatest-ever wins. It was a superb win for all of us.

But the good fortune didn't stop there. A couple of days later; I got the yellow jersey for myself, and then later, on Stage 16, I won my first individual stage.

On Stage 7, two days after surprising just about everybody by winning the team time trial, I covered an attack by French star Laurent Jalabert. Now "Jaja" had already won the stage into Verdun, and although he was near the end of his career, he was still a big-name rider. Stuey was still in yellow, so my job was to follow attacks. But all of a sudden, I was in a breakaway with Laurent Jalabert, and he was gunning for another stage win. By the end of the stage, we still had about a two-minute lead on the peloton, and I knew then that I was going to take the jersey.

It was just amazing, me, Jensie, in yellow! But it was also confusing, because I had taken the jersey from Stuey, my friend and teammate.

Winning the yellow jersey is something no rider will ever forget. As soon as I crossed the line, everybody collapsed onto me. Until then, I was just this little-known German, and then, suddenly, I was at the center of the cycling world. All of a sudden, everyone was hugging me, tapping me on the shoulder, and laughing. I was giving interviews to television stations I'd never seen or heard of before, British TV, French TV, American TV. There were 5,000, maybe 10,000 people in and around the race, just waiting for me, just waiting for a moment to see the yellow jersey. But of those 10,000, maybe 9,500 had never heard my name before! Yet they were cheering for me because they knew that whoever was wearing the yellow jersey had to be good! It made me somebody. And things continued well after the finish. Heck, when I finally got back to the hotel, there was even a little local marching band playing for me!

But like I said, at the same time, it felt very weird taking the yellow jersey from my teammate. The team, though, wanted me to cover the breakaways, because there were some hills on the stage with a hard final, and we weren't sure if Stuart could stay with the pack on the climbs. With me in the break, though, it really helped our situation. Since it was clear that the break was going to stay away to the finish, none of the big riders attacked much in the final. As a result, Stuey was able to stay with the main bunch, while I took the yellow jersey.

It was the safest option for the team, but I absolutely felt guilty. So on the next day, when he won some time in some midrace bonus sprints and took the jersey back, I was quite happy, and even relieved. I was like, "I'm happy to have had the jersey for a day and can now give it back to you. It belongs more on your shoulders!"

You see, in my eyes, Stuey really deserved the jersey. He had placed well in the prologue and had been doing all those crazy bonus sprints all week long, just trying to win a second here or two seconds there. He had just been full gas all week, mixing it up in the final sprints of each stage, just full on!

I don't know if people really have any idea of how stressful and dangerous the final kilometers of a Tour de France stage can be. There are pileups everywhere! It's a NIGHTMARE! And all week long, Stuey was taking all kinds of risks as he tried to get and keep the yellow jersey. He was just so determined, and in my opinion, he deserved the yellow jersey more than I did. My road into the yellow jersey was much easier. I profited from the circumstances. So yeah, I felt relieved to give the jersey back to Stuey.

Nevertheless, 2001 was a great year. I had 11 wins altogether, including an individual stage win again later in the Tour de France. And I think it's safe to say that the "Jens Voigt style" of racing was well established by that time, because just about every one of those victories came in a long breakaway.

Early in my career, I became well aware of the fact that I couldn't outclimb guys like Marco Pantani because I weigh 78 kilos (172 pounds). Climbers like Pantani weigh maybe 25 kilos less, so there's physically no way I could climb with them. And I knew I couldn't sprint with guys like Mario Cipollini, so somewhere along the way, really early on, I understood that if I was going to do something in this sport, I needed to go for the breakaways.

Luck in cycling is way too rare. I understood that I had to force my own destiny. I understood that I had to create my own luck!

I remember what Chris Boardman told me in my first year at GAN. He said, "Jens, if you try to win, you might lose. But if you don't try to win, you'll lose for sure!" And those were words that I lived by. To many, my attacks often appeared suicidal. And they were, really, because, well, when you go in an early break, the odds are never on your side.

I'd always preferred to have that little chance, that little possibility, that hope, on my side. By far, that was better than just going to the start line and basically telling myself that I was going to be beaten! Of course, there are days like that, when you just don't feel good, and you know that you're going to be pack fodder. But I certainly didn't want to spend my whole career like that! I wanted to be part of it. I wanted to put my stamp on the sport. And after a few successes in the early breakaways, I realized that this was what I was good at. This was what I liked doing. And I realized that it was interesting for the public, the journalists, and the sponsors, too. Before long, the Jensie in me was born!

FRIENDS ALONG THE WAY

"Wow! That's not human.
Stuey is not human. He's just wow!"

Jens as seen by Thor Hushovd (former teammate and world champion):

In cycling, there's a real hierarchy, and mostly the big riders only talk to the good riders. But that was never the case with Jens. When I first came on the Crédit Agricole team in 2000, Jens was already a well-established rider who was getting good results. But with him, there were no barriers. Jens talked to everyone, even neo-pros and *stagiaires* like me.

And let me tell you, it helps a young rider so much to get some attention and respect from the established riders. It helps them feel more secure. Straightaway I liked Jens. He was the guy I could always call for advice.

Like Jens, I moved to Toulouse to live and train because there were so many Crédit Agricole riders in the area. And there, too, I looked to Jens. Some of the guys could really party. For the

> Australians living there, it just seemed to be part of their culture. But Jens knew how to draw the line. He could go to a party and just drink one beer. I was a young rider. I didn't want to party. I wanted to win; I wanted to succeed as a cyclist. Jens showed me the way. He helped me navigate my way through those early years. He was my big brother.

ONE OF THE GREAT THINGS ABOUT CYCLING IS ALL THE GREAT FRIENDS YOU MEET OUT ON THE ROAD. And for me, many of them came while I was riding for GAN and Crédit Agricole. Perhaps it was because this was where I got my start in cycling's big time, or perhaps it's because I moved down to Toulouse to live and train with the boys. Little matter—many lifelong bonds were formed here with this French team.

As I've mentioned, when I first arrived to the team, Chris Boardman was the top dog. He had broken the world hour record and was one of the world's absolute best time trial riders. And he was very British! Be it his humor or the way he looked at things, you could just see that he was British. We often roomed together and had a lot in common. He, too, was a big reader and family man. At the time, he had four kids. It took me a while to catch up with him on that score—and actually I never quite did—but family was important to both of us.

We would spend hours talking. It was obvious that he came from a capitalist environment, compared to me, and saw life from that perspective. And we had long talks about the role of the welfare state. I, of course, had grown up believing that it was good, while he grew up in England during the Thatcher years in a time when the welfare state was being called into question and reshaped.

He was very interested in what it was like growing up in East Germany and how we trained, and I would try to learn from him in terms of technology, ergonomics, and so on. He was one of the first riders to really exploit the new watt-based SRM training that was first being developed in the 1990s. Chris was always looking at our sport from outside the box. He was always in pursuit of efficiency. Everything he did on or off the bike that had to do with cycling was centered on efficiency.

Now I was still sometimes in my East German mind-set. I was brought up to believe that the more kilometers you ride in training, the better you will be. I would come back from a long ride and say, "Oh, Chris, I just had a great five-hour ride with the boys. I loved it!"

And he would be like, "No, I hate that! I'd rather do two hours with some full-gas intervals and go home after three hours, you know, move on to other things!"

Chris was a real iconoclast in his day, a bit of an outsider. But in today's high-tech, neoscientific era of cycling, I think he would have fit right in. He often said, "I may not be the biggest talent, but I'm going to try to make the most out of the talent I've got." And in many ways, his entire career was like that. He didn't have a long career, only eight years, but he sure left his mark. He had a personal coach, when most riders didn't, and his training was always very focused. In addition, he examined all aspects of the sport: aerodynamics, diet, you name it. He was so analytical that he could look at your plate and tell you how many calories were on it. And he was the first person to give me a real, proper warm-up program before a time trial. Really, when it came to performance, he left no stone unturned. In many ways, Chris was already doing what teams such as CSC, HTC, and Sky did in later years.

It's funny. Chris was my teammate for only a couple of years, but he had a huge impact on me. And in some ways, that impact lasted until the end of my career, because it was Chris who gave me the idea to go finish my career with the hour record. That's exactly what he did, and I always thought, "Wow! What a great way to go out in style!"

And then, of course, there was Stuey O'Grady. He had already been on the team for a couple of years when I joined GAN, but he had turned professional at a very young age and was actually younger than me. He, too, lived in Toulouse, so we trained together plenty. And as it turned out, he was on the team with me for the entire 6 years I was with GAN and Crédit Agricole, and we hooked up again later on CSC.

Now Stuey was a true Aussie. And like all the Australian cyclists, he knew how to both work hard and play hard. He could really drink like a fish, but he could also slay himself on the bike! But unlike Chris, Stuey was not so analytical. He was more like me in that regard, more intuitive about training. If he needed to do some intervals, he would go out and do some hard intervals. But he wouldn't stay up the night before debating whether he should do one-minute intervals or two-minute intervals. No, that wasn't his style. He was more like, "As long as I go hard and make the legs hurt, that's good training." He was just a badass. I mean it as the highest compliment when I say that he was a freak of nature! They absolutely don't make them like Stuey anymore. When he retired, they just broke the mold, because you cannot make another Stuey! The way he could party so hard and perform hard at the same time was just unbelievable. Sometimes he would be seriously suffering from sleep deprivation and would still pull out these amazing performances. He was one of a kind! So many times I said, "Wow! That's not human. Stuey is not human. He's just wow!" He had this amazing ability to push through pain. He definitely came from the "Shut Up, Legs" school of suffering, perhaps even before me!

Stuey was pretty much the opposite of another great friend, my best friend, really, Bobby Julich. Bobby was much more like Chris Boardman. He could spend an entire evening or afternoon thinking about which interval would be best for his current fitness level. He could spend hours reading SRM files and data. But Bobby understands it all, and that's probably one of the reasons that he's become one of the best trainers in the sport following his retirement in 2008.

Sometimes, even often, we would butt heads. I would be like, "Bobby, be spontaneous! Go out there and have fun. Just get out there and smash the competition. Don't think about it all the time!" I would have the same conversations with Boardman. I would tell him, "Chris, stop thinking about how to be most efficient. Just go out there and race!" Sometimes guys like Chris and Bobby overthought things and ended up making mistakes because they asked too many questions. Boardman, for example, would attack in the final. But he would attack too soon, say five or six kilometers from the finish. I would say to him, "Chris, you're the world hour record holder! You can do four kilometers back-to-back in four minutes and sixteen seconds. No three teams together can do that! So just wait until the last three kilometers. If you get five seconds, they'll never catch you! Why attack from so far out?"

Yet despite our differences on the bike, Bobby and I hit it off from the moment we met. I'll never forget our first meeting. It came before we were even teammates, back in my first year as a pro with GAN. I was racing in the Paris-Nice race, my first big race, really. And I was pretty nervous. Bobby was on the rival French team, Cofidis. He was already a confirmed rider. He already had some big results, and he came up to me that day and said, "Calm down! You're making everybody nervous the way you're fighting for position all the time."

And I was like, "Hey, I just have a shit one-year contract. I have to prove that I'm good. I don't have two years to prove myself like all the other neo-pros."

And he was like, "Just chill, man. You're a good rider. Save your energy for when it counts."

Despite what could best be described as an awkward introduction, we had a lot in common. We're basically the same age, and once he came to the team, it became obvious that we had a lot of similar interests. I don't know if there was ever this key quintessential moment that made us best friends forever, but we are! We're so different, but we always complemented each other and challenged each other. Bobby always used to give me shit about stretching, or more appropriately, the fact that I didn't stretch. And I would just say, "Oh man, you and your stretching. You just make me nervous." I would be there playing Game Boy and he would be reading books on stretching or how to become a better public speaker, or something equally useful. He would have all this equipment for stretching or working his core muscles. I would say, "Bobby, half your suitcase is just for stretching. Man, just lie on your back and chill out." But he was never into that!

But as with Boardman, we could talk endlessly. We would compare his stories about growing up in America to mine about growing up in East Germany. And as an American living in Europe, he was fascinated by history. I remember racing in the Tour of Germany once; we raced past this castle, and I said, "Hey, Bobby, see that castle? That's where Martin Luther was once a prisoner. And, oh yeah, by the way, Martin Luther translated the Bible from Latin to German, and by doing so pretty much established the modern German language."

And Bobby was like, "Oh man, how cool is that!" And later, after the race, he asked me a million questions about it, and I told him everything I knew about Luther's 95 Theses and how he got excommunicated and all that.

Bobby was also curious about what life was really like in East Germany, about the education system, and just generally how things worked. And I was always asking him about American history. I was curious about what really happened to the American Indians or about the civil rights movement. Were Indians really still living on reservations today? What was the situation with blacks and whites today in America? Or how did you play this game of baseball? This was before races like the Tour of California or the Tour of Colorado existed and gave me a chance to see America with my own eyes. I learned a lot about life in America from Bobby.

And, of course, we would talk about cycling. I didn't have the energy or patience to study and analyze the sport like he did, but I still learned from him. Bobby is the one who taught me how to use an SRM system. He was the first person who taught me to alternate training between really hard and really easy. Until I met Bobby, I had always mixed up intervals during a training ride. And in-between intervals I would still be cruising around at 35 kph (22 mph). Bobby was the first to break it down, to do intervals at 100 percent but also rest and recuperate at 100 percent. That was something we did a lot more when I joined the CSC team, but Bobby was already on to it.

So I learned from him and, yes, we really complemented each other. But, mostly, I think we just clicked because, despite the fact that he grew up in America and I grew up in East Germany, we had similar values. Loyalty is important to both of us, being loyal to the team and your teammates. We both have families, and we're both trying to raise our kids in what we think is the right way. We are both curious people who like to broaden our horizons. We both like to see, talk about, and read about new things.

And it was during the two years we spent on Crédit Agricole that we started a little tradition that we continue up to this day. Bobby has lived in Nice for years, and so any year we're both in Nice for the finish of Paris-Nice, I spend the final night with him and his wife, Angela, and their kids, for a Mexican night where we make burritos and margaritas. We started doing this more than 15 years ago, but it's such a great tradition between us that we won't stop it!

Thor Hushovd was another key teammate in my Crédit Agricole years. He was younger and came on a little later. Now with Thor, things were a little different, because he came on as a neo-pro, and I was one of his mentors. Chris Boardman once told me that cycling goes in circles. "When you first come onto a team, you're young and others have to help you out," he said. "Then there's a period where you're on top. You're selfish. You want the team behind you. You want the special team. You want to win! But then at the end of the circle, it's up to you to help others, because it's time to give back and help the next kid fulfill his circle." And that's the way it was immediately with Thor. I wanted to help him out right away. I could tell he had what it took to become a good rider and all he needed was a helping hand and somebody to tell him how things work.

I think the first race we did was Paris-Bourges, a sort of warm-up for Paris-Tours, the race where I signed my first contract with the team. He was just a *stagiaire,* an apprentice, at the time. All of a sudden, the weather changed, and it started raining. He wasn't ready for that and didn't have any rain gear. So I went back to the team car and got him a rain jacket and some arm warmers and gloves. He was so happy that an experienced pro would actually help him out, but for me, it was just one of those moments when I could start giving back.

You could see immediately that he was a good, strong rider and just needed a little help and advice. I mean, after all, he was world time trial champion as an amateur and just bubbling with talent.

But what impressed me from the start with Thor was that, despite how young he was, he had a real plan. When he was 18, he already owned a Porsche and a nightclub. He was always clever with money.

He was sort of the picture-book Viking. He was big and strong and possessed such acute mental focus. That was one of his nicknames, "The Viking," and he lived up to it. He really was "The God of Thunder and Lightning"! He performed really well in the rain and descended like nobody else, maybe the best I've ever seen. Stuart O'Grady was probably as fast in the descent because he was just fearless, but Thor would take these corners so fast that it would take your breath away. And he would be like, "Oh, that was easy!"

We used to have this running gag where he would blow past me on a descent and then turn around and wave to me: "Come on, Jens! Hurry up!" But there was no way I could follow him on a descent. All I could do was wait until we started climbing the next mountain. And then I could ride along next to him and go, "Hey, you little fat sprinter! Who's suffering now, ha-ha!"

We became such good friends on the team that I asked him to be my best man, along with Jens Wichmann, an old friend from sports school, when Stephanie and I finally got married in 2003. And what a champion! He had lots of results all the time. He was a great world champion because, well, he just kept winning, which doesn't happen often. More times than not, it's very hard for world champions to win many races, because they're so marked with the rainbow jersey on their back. They just stand out. But Thor won two stages in the Tour de France and wore the yellow jersey that year. Talk about results! To me, he's one of the all-time greats. He was as strong as a horse, clever, fearless on the descents, and a very fast sprinter.

It's just a shame that he wasn't himself the last two years of his career. He caught this virus, and it took forever to find out what it was and what to do about it. It was very hard for him to regain his old form after that. Thor and I talked about it during our last years together in the peloton. He'd say, "Jens, it's so frustrating for me! I want to attack. I know when to go. But my body shuts me down!" On another occasion he'd come to me and say, "Jens, I just don't know how you do it. I can't imagine racing for another seven years." Thor is seven years younger than me, but he started his professional career at a lot younger age than I did, and he immediately became a lot more successful than I ever was.

I remember that he finished strong and with some really great stage finishes in one of his last races, the Arctic Race of Norway. Also I remember him becoming the first Norwegian rider to wear the yellow jersey in the Tour de France, as well as winning a classic like the 2009 Omloop Het Nieuwsblad, and 10 stages in the Tour de France. What I love about Thor is that we still chat and keep in contact, sending Christmas greetings to each other. He has not only been a champ on the bike but he is a great character off the bike, too, and a true friend for life.

Finishing up on the Hautacam climb after one of my better days in the Pyrenees—it was a great team ride where we helped set up our teammate Carlos Sastre for victory in the 2008 Tour de France. (James Startt)

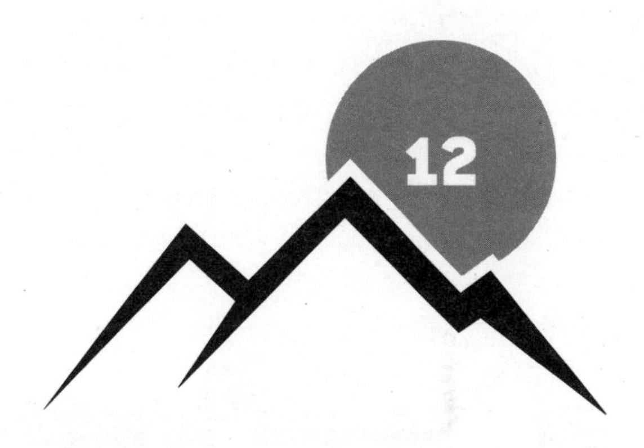

MOVING TO CSC

"Here on this team, I don't want to just make you better bike riders. I strive to make you better human beings."

Jens as seen by Francis Bur (soigneur for Voigt at GAN and Crédit Agricole, currently works for Team IAM):

Jens for me goes down as one of the four or five greatest champions I ever had the chance to work with. And over the years, I had the pleasure to work with plenty. There was Gilbert Duclos Lassalle (two-time winner of Paris-Roubaix), who was just amazing for his longevity. There was Greg LeMond, who was such a classy champion. Chris Boardman was just amazingly professional, not to mention very forward thinking with his very scientific approach. And then there's Jens, who was probably the most generous champion I ever met. What a big heart! When he came on the team, I spoke some German, but he insisted on speaking French because he wanted to integrate; he really wanted to be part of the team. He did everything 110 percent. You can't not love him! He gives everything he has every day on a bike. He never calculated anything on a bike or off!

That's why he was such a good team captain. He could do the work all day and still finish in the top 20. He could lead by example.

But Jens never impressed me more than in his last race with

Crédit Agricole in 2003. Nothing summed up his spirit better. We were at the Paris-Bourges classic, a late-season classic. What a day! But who would ever have guessed? At the start of the race, at the team meeting, he said, "Look, guys, it's been a long season, and this is my last race with the team. I don't have the legs to do much today, but I will do what I can to help you. I'll do my best early in the race and cover any breaks." Now, from all my years working in cycling, I know that when a rider has signed a contract with another team and is leaving at the end of the season, his motivation is never high. The last race is more of a formality.

Anyway, attacks started early, and for the first 25 kilometers, Jens did what he said he would do. He followed every move until he just couldn't go with any more accelerations.

And just after that, a breakaway finally got away without him or anybody from the team. Boy, was he pissed! He'd covered every move for the better part of an hour, and when a move finally got away, there wasn't one Crédit Agricole rider who could cover it. To make matters worse, most of the guys just plain dropped out that day. But not Jens. He wanted to be a professional until the end and respect the team colors until the final race was finished.

But in what can only be described as the irony of sports, Jens not only finished the race, but he got in a late-race counterattack, bridged up to the break, and won. He won the last race he ever rode for the team! That just doesn't happen. But it happened with Jens. Everybody else was in the showers. He should have been in the showers, but instead he was on the victory podium. The others came to the race to perform, and they were in the showers. Jens didn't come to the race trying to get a result, and he won! It's the most beautiful farewell anybody can give to a team.

AFTER SIX YEARS WITH ROGER LEGEAY, I DECIDED TO MOVE ON AND ACCEPT AN OFFER WITH THE DANISH CSC TEAM IN 2004. And almost immediately, I started another amazing six-year experience.

So many things that we take for granted now among the professional ranks were initiatives that found their start with CSC, one of the sport's truly revolutionary teams.

Bjarne Riis, a former Tour de France winner and general manager, was a pioneer in many ways because he looked at so many things besides riding bikes to build a great cycling team. He initiated survival training camps in the winter to build bonds with teammates. He was a maniac when it came to diet, and we were one of the first teams to have our own movable kitchen in a truck at all the big races. He was also a big advocate of cross-training and was one of the first to have his cyclists do core training in the gym. A lot of things that we take for granted today in professional cycling were first implemented by Bjarne.

Bjarne just took everything to another level, it seemed. I remember one year, he wanted to use Shimano for sponsorship and Shimano agreed, but they wanted to provide a whole package, including pedals and wheels. But Bjarne said, "No, your wheels aren't good enough for my team. We just want the group set." Shimano refused, so Bjarne said, "Okay, then I will buy the parts I want for the team." Then he went and bought the exact parts—what he considered the best parts—for the team's use. He didn't want to be forced into using inferior equipment just to please a sponsor. He wanted to use only the equipment that he thought was best for his team. He was one of the first managers to push for more independence when it came to equipment.

Bjarne also really tried to teach each rider to take more responsibility for himself and the team. He always surprised me and impressed me with his ability to take criticism. People on the team would sometimes be critical of a decision that he was making. Sometimes, they would say something like, "You know, Bjarne, that's a shit idea!"

But Bjarne never got mad; he never said, "Well, I'm the boss and that's the way it is." Instead, he always engaged in the dialogue. "Hmm, do you think so? What is it that's wrong? What do you think?"

That was a first for me. Until then, the team managers were always the boss, and you did what they said. Period.

But Bjarne was different. He questioned things and was willing to take risks. Perhaps the best example was in his survival camps or "team-building camps," as we called them, because they would build team spirit. I mean, first of all, he was taking a huge risk. After all, he had just spent five or six million euros on the salaries of some of the world's best cyclists, and then he was taking them out in the dark in Denmark in the middle of winter somewhere. Who knows what might happen? But he thought it was worth the risk, because those camps really served to bond us together. Let me tell you, you never forgot which person shared his last chocolate bar with you at four o'clock in the morning when you were guarding the fire on night watch. You remember those talks you had with the guys who were on watch duty with you. You remember that last little bit of chocolate.

Every December, we would venture off on these camps. We never knew exactly how long they would last or exactly where they would be. That was all part of it. Bjarne didn't like routine. And he liked to keep us on our toes. The first one was only 36 hours, but with no sleep and constant challenges.

At one camp, I remember, in the middle of the night we had to jump into this lake. It was pitch black out, and we didn't know how far we had to jump. The instructor just said, "Okay, boys, you can't see the water, but it's down there!" All we could see was a little fluorescent buoy. We had to jump down, swim to the buoy, and then swim down to the bottom of the lake and back up. We didn't really know how far the jump was. We just had to trust that there was water where they said there was water and that the landing was safe.

Another time, there were 10 of us at the bottom of this dry dam. And there was just a rope with a pulley. We had to pull each guy up, and then when there were about five guys already on the top, it was up to them to simply pull the others up one by one. There were always these sorts of activities, nonstop.

One time, I remember, we had three sailboats. And then when we

Even as a child, I never pretended that I was normal and certainly could never sit still! (Courtesy of Jens Voigt)

Sporting East German fashion on a summer holiday in the Elbsandsteingebirge Mountains near Dresden. Those old leather shorts sure were indestructable. (Courtesy of Jens Voigt)

Attracted to cycling at a young age, I prepare for a ride on a tricycle at my grandmother's house in the village of Schwanbeck, about three kilometers from our home in Dassow. (Courtesy of Jens Voigt)

Posing for a family picture in the old days. Boy, did those leather shorts get a lot of mileage! We would hand them down from one kid to the next, over the years. (Courtesy of Jens Voigt)

Here with my brother, Ronny (left), and my sister, Cornelia (center). Ronny is one of the big reasons I got into cycling. He was once a state champion in the kilometer event, something that inspired me to cycle myself. (Courtesy of Jens Voigt)

Ronny (left) and Cornelia (right) during a family visit while I was at sports school in Berlin in 1985. (Courtesy of Jens Voigt)

At the annual carnival party in 1986, on a Saturday night in Berlin, with friends from my sports school. (Courtesy of Jens Voigt)

Visiting my parents after a race in Hungary in 1988. You can see by the cycling cap that I was still a member of the East Germany cycling team. That shack in the background is where we built my parents' new house in 2002. (Courtesy of Jens Voigt)

Posing before the start of a stage in the Rheinland Pfalz Rundfahrt race in 1994. Despite having my best amateur season ever, I still could not get a contract with a professional team. (Courtesy of Jens Voigt)

Winning a stage with the German National team in the Rapport Tour in South Africa in 1996, my last year as an amateur. (Courtesy of Jens Voigt)

Sporting the colors of my first professional team ZVVZ-Giant in 1997. The team may have been short-lived, but it still had one of the coolest jerseys. (H. A. Roth)

Racing full speed with my mentor and friend Chris Boardman at the Breitling Grand Prix in 1999, a two-man time trial that we ended up winning. (H. A. Roth)

My parents holding my trophy and flowers after I won my first Critérium National in 1999. It would become my signature race, after I won it five times. (Courtesy of Jens Voigt)

My many jerseys hanging on the line to dry, after my mom cleaned them up. (Courtesy of Jens Voigt)

Standing in front of my parents' new house on Jens-Voigt-Ring, a house I built for them in 2002. (Courtesy of Jens Voigt)

In what was definitely one of my all-time great memories, here I am pacing my friend and teammate Bobby Julich up the Col d'Eze on the final stage of the Paris-Nice race in 2005. It was so satisfying to help Bobby hold onto the lead and secure one of his best victories ever. (James Startt)

were about a kilometer-and-a-half from shore, the military guy just said, "Okay, everybody in the water!" So, no questions asked, we just jumped into the water, and we were swimming around the boats a kilometer-and-a-half away from shore. Then they divided us into groups or teams of ten and threw each group a paddleboard with a couple of sets of flippers, and we had to get everyone back to shore. Now some guys, like our team director, Alain Gallopin, weren't the best swimmers. So we had to figure out what to do to get everyone back safely. I remember we put Alain on the board and made him our skipper. It was up to him to steer and give directions, and then we worked together to get back to shore. The weaker swimmers would hang onto the surfboard and paddle with their feet, and the better swimmers were on the outside with the flippers. Now the water was something like 500 meters deep there, but that's how we got ourselves back to shore.

Other activities were more fun. Once we did a 10-hour go-cart race in teams. Each team would swap the car among each other and try to get as many laps on the other teams as possible. That was fun! Another year we were in Denmark in the snow, and each team had a sled with all our supplies for making fires, sleeping, eating, you name it. We would have to pull the sled in the snow from one point to another, and then, at night, we just camped in the forest in the snow.

The main thing was that it always changed. Some years it was more about being competitive, while other years the camp focused more on staying together. But the camps were nothing if they weren't challenging. That was the bottom line: to take each person to their physical limits so we knew how each person would behave and react in a crisis situation.

Who is going to stick together? Who is going to break apart? Who is going to break down? Who is going to get stronger with the challenge? That way Bjarne knew what to expect from people when they were in extreme situations—which come up a lot in bike racing—because that's what happens when you get only two hours' sleep a night with next to no food or water. That's what happens when you're walking in some stupid dark forest at night, all night. People were exhausted. But they bonded. The team really bonded, because leaving somebody behind just wasn't an option.

And although I didn't realize it at the time, I think it's safe to say that my years in the old KJS Ernst Grube sports school in Berlin came in handy at those camps, because both represented a situation in which we had to pull together if we were going to make it. And let me tell you, at the end of each camp, we were proud. We always finished up with a big cookout, and after everyone took a 30-minute shower just to get warm, we had lots of great stories to tell. So the camps definitely served their purpose.

Sure, when we were in the middle of it all, when we were in the middle of some forest, there would always be a moment when we were like, "Bjarne! Why do we have to do this every year?" But in the end, we were always glad we did. We gained trust in each other and strengthened our friendships. And since the entire staff participated, we all grew together. We all became friends for life.

But what I remember most about the CSC years is the way Bjarne was able to get the best out of his riders. And that was never more true than with riders who were a bit older, like me, and whose careers were standing still a little bit or maybe even slowly beginning to decline. He was good at giving those riders that little kick. Look at what he did just a couple of years ago with Nick Nuyens. Nick was always a good, strong rider, but he went to work with Bjarne, and all of a sudden, he was a Tour of Flanders winner.

I'll never forget my first training camp with CSC in 2004. At one point, Bjarne gave a little talk, and at the end, he said, "Here on this team, I don't want to just make you better bike riders. I strive to make you better human beings. I want you to be more aware of what you're doing and why you're doing it."

I was like, "Wow, this is going to be different!" It was a big call. But to this day, in my eyes, I think Bjarne lived up to it.

Bjarne is good at giving you that little extra something. He's good at giving you that boost of confidence. I've often thought about what it is about Bjarne, and I guess the biggest thing is that he takes every rider seriously. He treats every rider like a grown-up man. He listens to your opinion. He uses your knowledge and what you tell him, your own experiences, to come up with the best program possible for each rider so that they make the most out of each race. But not only does he analyze your racing schedule, he looks at the way you race and where you best use your energy in a race, so that you can race more efficiently. When I first signed on with CSC, Bjarne was personally involved in each rider's training program and had his heart and soul involved in everything. That changed over the years, because the pressure of finding new sponsors and managing the team took up more and more of his time. But for a long time, Bjarne monitored every rider's training program. It was very personal.

One thing he did that I never saw on another team was rent a van for all the team directors. The van would follow us the whole day on our training rides. And inside the van, Bjarne was analyzing each rider with all the directors. Together they would break down each rider's technique, pedal stroke, and position. Was one rider sitting a little to the left or right? What kind of gears did they choose? For the entire ride, they discussed how each rider looked, what their training program was. Should this rider do more intervals? Should that rider raise his saddle a little more? No one thing in itself was enormous. He just looked at every detail about every rider and tried to make every detail as perfect as possible. But if a rider could gain just 1 percent in aerodynamics and say 2 percent in diet, well, when you add it all up, that could maybe amount to a 10 percent improvement. And that, my friends, is significant!

When I first came to CSC, Bjarne's approach was holistic. It wasn't just pedal harder, pedal faster. It was about looking at the whole picture. And it was a very novel approach to cycling. But it turned out to be very forward thinking, as later on, teams such as HTC and Sky employed similar approaches, and with great success, I might add.

That and the fact that Bjarne brought together a great bunch of guys really made for some great years.

Another success story was with my friend Bobby Julich. Bobby had really come to an end on the Telekom team. And when his contract wasn't renewed in 2003, it looked like he might even retire. Bobby was a little jaded after his years with Telekom. After all, the team was run by Germans, which I know something about! And they weren't going to say, "Okay, how do you feel, Bobby?" No. Instead, they were more like, "I pay you. Do your job!" And he didn't like that. He didn't need that.

So when Bjarne asked me what I thought about hiring Bobby, I said clearly, "Bobby is a very good rider. He just needs a little inspiration after the Telekom years."

And that's exactly what he got when he came to CSC. Bobby didn't cost Bjarne much, since he was facing an early retirement. And I think when Bobby came that first year, he wanted to see if he had any life still left in him as a professional cyclist. But he fit right in and had four great years with us, years that included winning races like Paris-Nice, so clearly there was a lot of cycling left in him. He just needed someone like Bjarne to pull the best out of him.

And for me, of course, I couldn't have been happier, because I got to have my best friend as my teammate once again. How great was that? In fact, the team saw how well we got along and worked together, and they made an exception and just let us always be roommates. That was not Bjarne's policy. As with training, he always liked to mix things up, and the rooming list always changed. But he let us stay together. I think Bjarne saw that by putting us together, he was guaranteed to have two experienced riders who had good morale, which is important for team dynamics, especially in longer races like the Tour de France. And Bobby and I, of course, were happy to be able to talk about family life, books, politics, economics, or whatever else in the evenings. We were really able to unwind. So it was a win-win situation for everyone.

I'll never forget the first year Bobby came to CSC, in 2004. He crashed out of the Tour de France in the time trial and was in the hospital, pretty banged up. That night after dinner, the team asked me if I wanted to go down to the hospital to see him. He was still pretty whipped out under anesthesia when we got there and was just out of it. I was standing there with him, and I said, "You know, I've been in some hospitals myself, and the one thing I remember is that the food is always shit, and there's never enough of it!" Now I know Bobby likes a good hamburger, so I said, "Why don't we just go down to McDonald's and get some burgers and fries, so when he does wake up, he has something to eat!" And that's what we did. Heck, we pretty much had to smuggle the burgers back into the hospital. He was still out when we got back, so we just left the bag of burgers and fries.

And the next morning, Bobby called and said, "Ah, you're the best! I woke up at two in the morning, and I was just starving. And then I started smelling those burgers and I was so-o-o happy!"

Bobby and I clicked so well. One time Bobby was sitting in the hotel restaurant during a training camp. He had already been there for a couple of days, and he didn't know when exactly I would arrive. But as soon as I walked into the restaurant, he just looked around. It was like he had a sixth sense that I was suddenly in the room. Trey Greenwood, who worked on the team, was with Bobby, and when he saw that, he just said, "Wow, I see what they mean about you two being like an old married couple!"

Savoring my third and final victory in the Tour de France. (James Startt)

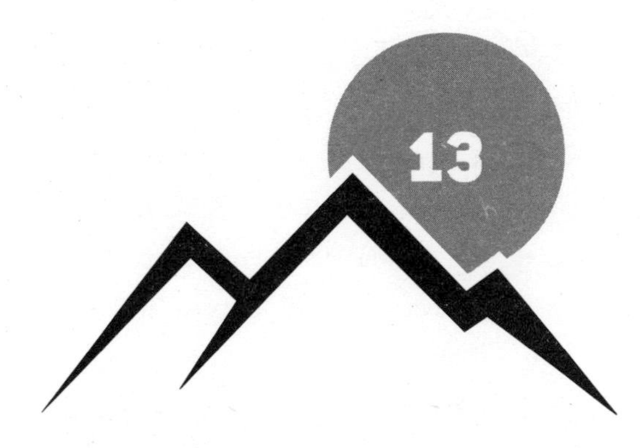

OPERATION PUERTO

"Just tear all those guilty riders out of the shadows and burn them!"

MY YEARS AT CSC WEREN'T ALWAYS FUN AND EASY. Our team, like many others, had run-ins with doping. The first year I rode for CSC, in 2004, Tyler Hamilton, who had been with the organization up until the year before, tested positive at the Olympics and at the Tour of Spain. And even though it happened when he was no longer a part of the program, the positive tests cast suspicion on us.

The worst moment, however, was still to come. Just before the 2006 Tour de France, our team leader, Ivan Basso, was expelled from the race for his involvement with Dr. Eufemiano Fuentes and the whole Operation Puerto investigation in Spain (although he was not prosecuted for doping).

To this day, I can still go for days or even a week without reading *Cyclingnews* or any of the other news outlets dedicated to bicycle racing. And the time before the 2006 Tour de France was one of those moments. I was just focused on all the last-minute preparations regarding the start of the Tour and hadn't kept up on the latest developments around Operation Puerto.

So I was really taken off guard once I got to Strasbourg, where the Tour was starting. As usual, we got there a couple of days early, and we were out on our last training ride with the team just the day before the start, when all of a sudden, Ivan stopped, jumped into a car, and drove off. We were just like, "What was that?"

Perhaps I should have known that something was up the day before, when at the press conference, a journalist asked, "Hey, Ivan, what's the name of your dog?"

I sat there thinking to myself, "What? I have dogs. One is named Jeannie. The other one is Inka. Why is that interesting? How is that relevant to the race?" I had no idea that the names of pets were being used as code words or something. And as the news continued to unfold, I was just blown away by the depth of the doping. There were apparently more than 200 athletes from all kinds of sports, tennis, soccer, you name it. And in that 200, there were some 55 cyclists. As the details came out regarding the depth and sophistication of the doping, I was shocked. Names started to surface—surprising names. Sometimes I'd just blurt out, "Him? He's not even a good rider. Why would he dope? What would he do without dope? Is he hopeless?" No, that was truly shocking! To see how deeply it went all across Europe.

In some ways, I felt like I was reliving the Festina affair. But in other ways, it was so much worse. When Festina hit, it was easy to rationalize it. I figured, "Well, they're doing what a lot of people are doing because these are bad times." But this was eight years later. Things were supposed to have improved! You could explain Festina by saying that the whole sport had fallen into a trap. But with Puerto, it was more like this whole evil empire, a real Mafia-style organization, had been built up to make money and give a few riders an unfair advantage. For me, at least, it was much worse. And for my own teammate to be involved was just devastating.

I, of course, was furious. And I was quoted largely in the press when I said, "Just tear all those guilty riders out of the shadows and burn them!" Although I wasn't thinking of Ivan when I said that. I think I actually said that before I knew Ivan had been questioned. That didn't go over too well, and I received a lot of criticism from fans and other riders, not to mention Ivan's lawyers. To be honest, Ivan was okay with my criticisms, but his lawyers and his fans sure weren't. And other riders and their fans didn't appreciate my comments either. Some people said, "Hey, why don't you just shut up and play it safe!" But there was no fucking safe playing here.

The press, naturally, liked that someone was speaking out, because it made for good copy. And some riders did come up to me and thank me for saying what I said. But they were also relieved that they didn't have to say it themselves.

The next year I got involved with the CPA, the Professional Cyclists Association, because I thought I could maybe help the sport. We worked on a lot of things, such as encouraging teams to have insurance for riders, and we lobbied for a minimum salary for neoprofessionals. But one of the biggest things we did was to put in place the biological passport that we use today to monitor a rider's biological levels over the years in order to determine if, perhaps, a rider has had an artificial boost. The biological passport allowed us to have indirect detection of doping in addition to the direct detection through drug controls. By monitoring each rider's values over the years, we could see more clearly if a rider was gaining an advantage from external means. We spent a lot of time establishing the list of which substances should be legal, which should not be permitted, and what levels of certain substances—say, for instance, caffeine—would be acceptable.

Or take cortisone, for example. Every human body possesses natural levels of cortisone. But if someone takes cortisone externally, the body will actually reduce its own production. So if you see a rider's natural cortisone drop significantly, he is very likely taking cortisone externally. There's really no other way to explain it.

Unfortunately, what I learned most about working on the CPA was that I'm not a politician. I like to make 100 percent of the people happy, and as a politician, that just isn't possible. Some people criticized me for pushing too far forward, while others criticized me for not doing enough. "Why did you stop halfway, Jens? Why didn't you go all the way?" I was in between, and frankly, sometimes, I felt like I was the only one standing up in the middle of a battlefield. Everybody else was in their trenches, firing. And I was standing all alone between them, vulnerable. It was bad! It was really an ungratifying job, and I didn't smile too much while I was doing it! As a result, I think it's safe to say that politics will not be a career option for me after cycling.

But I can tell you that as far as I was concerned, I never had a single conversation about doping with Bjarne or any member of the team. At CSC, we even had a clause in our contracts specifying that doping, or anything that was perceived to have put the team's livelihood in danger, would result in immediate suspension. Bjarne and our team even campaigned with the International Cycling Union and race organizers to cut down on the race kilometers. He wanted to make stages shorter and generally less difficult because, well, it wasn't the early 1990s, when people used to race on "super petrol," anymore. If the racing wasn't as demanding, riders would be less tempted to go back to doping just to survive.

Now I know about Tyler, of course, and I know that he wrote a book in which he claimed that Bjarne did this and that with him. Bjarne was accused of knowing about Ivan's meeting with Fuentes, although he denied it. And to be honest, I never did ask him up-front about what may or may not have happened. It's ironic, really, but none of us wanted to touch the subject. We were all just so focused on doing the best we could and doing so in a proper manner. I mean, we could read what we wanted in the newspapers or on the Internet. And really no one on the team showed any interest in bringing up the subject.

And personally, I just didn't see a need to make things more complicated. There was a part of me that just didn't want to know about everything that may or may not be going on in the sport. You know what they say: Ignorance is bliss. But part of it was also a way to protect myself, because I never wanted to get into a situation where I started to think that every rider who ever beat me was on drugs. Call it a survival tactic, if you will. But if you think that you're always getting beat by drug cheats, then why continue racing? Obviously, I rode through some pretty dark years in cycling. But those of us who wanted to race with dignity had to focus on the positive. We had to believe that winning clean was possible. But if you spend all your time reading or thinking about all the details surrounding every rider who gets caught doping, it will just eat away at you. I didn't want to poison my soul thinking about it. Those thoughts can become a cancer all their own. You can't ignore it entirely, but you can't let the suspicion and all these evil thoughts control your life. I refused to let that happen to me.

I knew riders who, as soon as someone got half a wheel in front of them, would go, "Oh no, what is he on?" I always preferred to think that the guy in front of me was just pushing the pedals a little bit harder than I was.

All I can say is that, for me, there was never a hint of doping on Bjarne's team. Never once did someone say, "You know, maybe, Jens, you could use a little help?" No, that never happened. Not even in code words, not even once! At least not to me. And you can give me a lie detector test or put me in front of a grand jury; the answer would be the same. I was never approached about doping while I was on Bjarne's team. Furthermore, I always had the impression that Bjarne liked my attitude toward doping. He liked that I was outspoken about the issue.

It has been widely reported and written over the years that some riders were open with their teammates about their doping and that there was real complicity between some riders when it came to taking drugs. Some guys who have come out and admitted to taking drugs try to make it look like everybody knew about drug use and everybody was in the same boat.

No, everybody was *not* in the same boat! I've sometimes used the example that if you're not paying your taxes or if you're cheating on your wife, you're not going to tell everybody. You know it isn't right, so you're going to keep it a secret as much as possible. And it's the same with doping. If somebody is going to try to gain an advantage over their competition or maybe even their own teammates, do you think they're going to tell everybody about it? No, of course they're not going to share that information. I can tell you that no one ever came to me saying, "Come to Madrid. Come to Puerto. We're going to sit around and change blood, and then we're going to make millions!" No, no one ever said this to me! It just wasn't like that! I think the people who were doing illegal or just plain dangerous things were keeping that behavior as secret as possible. So everybody didn't know everything about everybody.

I can only imagine that some riders must have seen each other in the waiting room of Dr. Fuentes's office. And some must have thought, "Okay, I'm paying this guy 10,000 or maybe 15,000 euros a year to give me an advantage. But if he's taking the same from each rider, then we're all getting the same advantage. So, in the end, there is no advantage. In the end, we're all on the same level. So why am I paying him all this money just to get the same treatment?"

I'm sure that to this day there are still people who are convinced that I was doing the same thing as some others, and I just hid it better. What can I say to that? Do you think my doctor sits on the moon? I just don't think you can really hide a sophisticated doping program today. They can check my bank account, my passport. There are no records of any trips to Madrid, no records of trips in which I flew to and from some place in the same day. There's nothing like that. About the only bank transfer I have made in the last few years was a 5,000-euro loan to my brother to help him buy a car for his own little company that he was starting up. Except for that, I have made no bank transfers.

The most important thing is that the people you know trust you and believe in you, and you have to trust yourself. Often I'm my own hardest critic. Okay, often I'm my biggest fan, too! But I can also be my hardest critic. And at the end of the day, I have to look at myself in the mirror and be satisfied with what I see.

Bobby Julich and I would sometimes talk about the state of doping, and we were both just so much happier feeling like the playing field was becoming more even. And whenever somebody would test positive, boy, that just really bummed us out. We would say, "Oh man, I thought this was stopping!" But at the same time, we were both relieved to see that the controls were improving, that the biological passport was working. In addition, we were committed to leading by example and setting a good example for the young riders coming into the sport.

A few times, as one of the oldest riders on the team, I was asked to speak at the first training camp of the year. And I'd always say, "I don't know what you have heard or what you think, but doping on this team is a no-go!" I would reiterate that we all needed to be fully aware that if any one of us made a mistake, that person would be putting the livelihood of everyone on the team in jeopardy. So doping was just a no-go. Not even a little bit. It's like being pregnant. You can't be just a little pregnant, and you can't just take a little bit of dope. I remember saying to them, "Listen to me! If I catch any of you doing it, I will hold you personally responsible for the damage you do to the team. If things turn out really bad, I will come and burn your house down! I will personally come to your place and burn your house down!"

I was so adamant because, at the time around Operation Puerto, cycling had lost all trust. Fans didn't trust us. The media didn't trust us. And sponsors all had clauses in their contracts stipulating that they could pull out immediately in the event of a positive drug test. So I wasn't exaggerating. One person's mistake really could bring down the whole team!

Yes, we did talk about doping in team meetings, but we talked about the fact that it was just not an option on our team. That much we talked about.

It was soon after Puerto that Bjarne even reached out to Rasmus Damsgaard, a member of Anti-Doping Denmark and one of his most ardent critics. And what did Bjarne do? He offered Damsgaard carte blanche with regard to dope testing on our team. He let Damsgaard know that he could come test us as much as he wanted, whenever and wherever he wanted, so that he could see that we were doing the right thing and there was no doping whatsoever on our team. Damsgaard accepted Bjarne's offer and proceeded to set up this whole whereabouts system much like the World Anti-Doping Agency (WADA) does today. It was Damsgaard's system, and he could come and test any of us whenever he wanted.

I remember it well because he had this assistant, and boy, did she travel! Damsgaard really wanted to catch somebody to prove that he was right and that our sport was really full of doping. So he would be testing us two, maybe three times a week in the beginning, in an effort to catch us by surprise. He also wanted to catch anybody who might be thinking that since they were just tested one day earlier, for example, they could take a substance and have time for it to leave their system before the next test. I remember one day I was at a wine-tasting party at a friend's hour drinking some *Glühwein*, a holiday wine served warm with spices, when I got a call for a test. We were just sitting with friends having a barbecue and tasting wine when I got the call. The testers came to the house, and I did a doping test right there in the house, and my friends were all like, "Geez, Jens, your sport is fucked up!" Ha-ha, what can I say? It was all for a good cause!

Most important, though, Damsgaard came away from the experience believing that CSC was all right. But that was pure Bjarne.

Damsgaard was not our friend. In fact, he was quite the opposite. But Bjarne just invited him into the team and gave him unfettered access because he knew we had nothing to hide.

So, personally, I only have good things to say about Bjarne and his program. I'll never forget what he did after my bad crash in the 2009 Tour de France. I was lying in bed in the hospital between surgeries, and Bjarne called me up. He was getting married in about two days' time, but he took the time to call me. He said, "Jens, don't worry, you will have a contract next year. You get your surgery done and come back happy and healthy, and I promise you that we will have a contract for you. Don't worry about a thing. The next time we see each other, we'll sign it. But don't stress. It's a promise between us. You're safe. You have a future. I know you're strong. I know you will come back, so I want you to know that you have a contract." And that's exactly what happened. That's the way Bjarne always was in my eyes—fair and correct.

That doesn't mean that we never disagreed, though. We did.

We had a couple of arguments over the years. One of the biggest came during the 2006 Giro d'Italia, when I gave a stage away. I had gotten in a breakaway on Stage 19 with Juan Manuel Gárate, and because of the race situation, I had been sitting on the break all day without pulling. This was the year when my teammate Ivan Basso won the race, and he was in the pink jersey. It's common for a support rider like me not to pull in a breakaway situation.

At the team meeting that morning, in fact, Bjarne had asked me to cover the breakaways. There was an uphill finish that day, so the tactic was for me to get in a break. That way, if the race exploded on the final climb, I would be able to help Ivan once the leaders caught up to us. But on that day, the breakaway stayed away. From the get-go, I told the guys in the breakaway that I couldn't pull because I was just there for Ivan. But I also told them clearly that I would not go for victory at the end of the day. And throughout the entire stage, the others in the break never once gave me a bad look or anything. But then, at the end of the day, there were only two riders left, Juan Manuel Gárate and me, and I think Bjarne got a bit excited when he saw the break was going to stay away, and I actually had a good chance to win. But I wasn't going to go back on my word after everyone else had done all the work all day. At different times during the day, I asked Bjarne, "Hey, can I work just a little so that if we do go to the line, I can go for the stage win?" But all day long, Bjarne was adamant: "No, just wait. Do nothing!"

So in the end, I came up to Gárate and said to him, "Hey, this is your win. There will be no trouble from me. You win, and I will be second." But just then, Bjarne was on the radio, saying, "Okay, Jens, everything is cool in the peloton. Ivan still has two teammates. There is no trouble here, so you can go for the stage win."

And I was just like, "No, Bjarne, I just told Juan Manuel that it's his win. I can't change that." Bjarne really wanted the victory, but I refused. "No, no, Bjarne," I said. "I will not change my position on this one. I will not win this stage!"

Bjarne was like, "Come on, Jens, I really want you to win this stage! You can do it!" But I would not.

I said to him very bluntly, "Bjarne, there just is no honor in it!"

Back on the team bus, Bjarne was still mad about the lost opportunity, but then, the next morning, after he had time to think about it, he came back to me and said, "Jens, that's great! That's what I want to see on my team! That was a good example of leadership. I was wrong yesterday."

You know it's not easy for a team manager to admit he was wrong, but Bjarne had that capacity. So really, to this day, I have nothing but respect for Bjarne.

While I was on CSC, my style of racing also changed. I didn't have to rely only on my suicide break tactics. I could also just flat out win races such as the Tour of Bavaria, the Tour of Germany, the Tour of Denmark, the Mediterranean Tour. And, of course, when you're looking to win the overall, you don't go into the suicide breakaways anymore. I was the leader for the smaller and medium races, but when the team had real Tour de France contenders like Carlos Sastre or Frank and Andy Schleck, my ability to ride for myself in the world's biggest races was reduced. But I was always okay with that. That was never frustrating for me. It's also very rewarding to work hard and see a guy like Carlos winning, or guys like Frank or Andy on the podium in a race such as the Tour de France.

As you get older, you come to realize that sports, like life, are not just all about me, me, me! It's not just about winning, winning, winning. And in bicycle racing, you start asking yourself, "Okay, how can I improve the status of the team? How can I help my friend to win?" In moments like that, you have to sacrifice your own chances of victory. And to get there, you have to go through the process. You have to grow up and grow into it. But for me, at least, that transition came easily.

Although it did not come naturally, I, too, eventually embraced high-tech training methods.

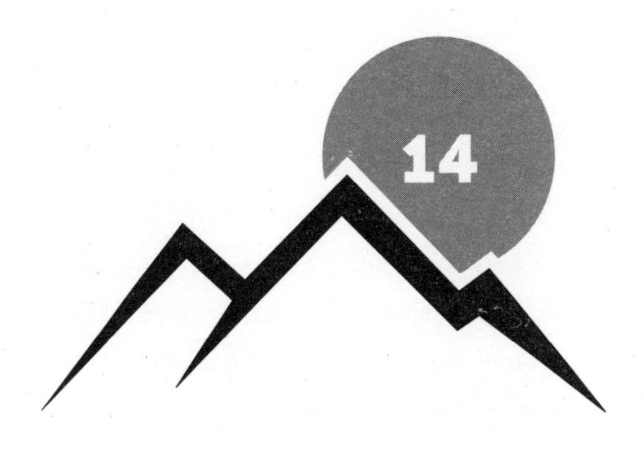

TRAINING

"Training hard is easy.
But training smart is the hard part!"

BICYCLE RACING WENT THROUGH SO MANY CHANGES IN THE 25 YEARS I RACED AS A TOP AMATEUR AND PROFESSIONAL. But, undoubtedly, some of the greatest changes came in training.

Training in East Germany was different in many ways from the way I approached the sport as a professional. Part of it was simply that, as a young amateur, I didn't race nearly as frequently as I did once I turned professional. But mostly, what I remember about training as an East German was the long, slow distance, the LSD, as it's called. We just rode so many kilometers! Sure, we did some intervals when we were getting ready for a big race, but mostly our training just centered on building power and strength by spending a maximum amount of time on the bike.

Heck, I remember endurance tests where we did a series of three-day training blocks. The objective was to see how far we could push our bodies before they were breaking down more than they were building strength. Recuperation is a key element in training, and the coaches were trying to see just how much stress the body could endure before it absolutely needed to recuperate. We would do 180 kilometers, 200 kilometers, 220 kilometers in the first three-day block, followed by one day of rest. Then we would do 200 kilometers, 220 kilometers, and 250 kilometers with one day off. Then we did 250 kilometers, 280 kilometers, and 300 kilometers with one day off. Then we did 280 kilometers, 300 kilometers, and finally 330 kilometers. Do you know what time we had to get up in the morning to ride 330 kilometers? And we weren't riding fast. This was all LSD, long and slow. Now, LSD is great in some ways. It really makes you strong. But it also makes you slow.

Of course, we had a lot of good results with that system, and East Germany was a strong cycling country. But we really had only a couple of big objectives each year in races such as the Peace Race or the world championships. As a result, the training was just very labor intensive. It wasn't like in the professional ranks, where you can be racing every weekend and you have objectives all year long. When you have a Tour of Flanders one Sunday and Paris-Roubaix the next, you're just not going to have the time or energy to do a couple of six-hour rides in-between, because when you're not racing full gas, you're trying to recover from racing full gas.

My first real exposure to a more progressive approach to training came when I started working with Heiko Salzwedel on the ZVVZ-Giant team. Now Heiko may have come from the East German system like I did, but he was a track coach, and to this day, he is one of the most respected cycling coaches when it comes to the track. I think he has won world championship titles with at least four different countries. He produced world champions when he worked with East Germany, Australia, and Denmark as well as the Great Britain team and Team

Sky. He worked very closely with Bradley Wiggins when he broke the hour record.

As a track coach, he had a very different approach to cycling than my previous coaches, who were more road oriented. He was the first coach who talked to me about keeping a high pedal cadence and spinning my legs more. And his approach to speed and endurance was quite novel. He really separated working speed and working endurance. When we were working on speed with Heiko, we would do very short intervals at high intensity. But then when we worked on endurance, we really rode long, and it was not uncommon for us to go out and do 250 kilometers in a day.

He also was experimental. He believed that the body should go through all its physical zones, from resting to a full-out effort, before breakfast. So sometimes, we would get up at six in the morning and go out for a ride. It would be short, but it would force the body through all its zones. We would ride easily for say 10 minutes, then pick it up. We would do medium intervals, higher intervals, and finally finish with full-out sprints. It might take only 45 minutes, but it prepared the body for the real workout later in the day.

My training took an even bigger jump, however, when I moved to the GAN team in 1998. There, for the first time, the team had a full-time trainer. Heiko was a great trainer, but because the team was on a small budget, he also had to be the general manager and the race director. On GAN, we had one person, Denis Roux, who was a full-time trainer, and he really helped me take my training to the next level.

Denis sat me down and said, "Your training has to be different now. You're not getting dropped because you can't race for five hours at 42 kilometers an hour. You're getting dropped because you can't do 55 or 60 kph for 10 minutes!" Denis understood that with all my base training from the East German days, I had enough endurance to last me a lifetime. What I needed was to train to sustain more intense efforts and be able to recover more quickly from the lactic acid created by those efforts. Bicycle racing is all about strength and recovery. Riders who can make the biggest efforts and recover fastest are the ones who will be at the front and in the breakaways the most.

So with Denis I really started training for bigger efforts and faster recovery. I remember doing these two-hour home trainer programs. Denis was one of the first coaches to actually replace road rides with home trainer workouts, because you can train more specifically. Mentally, it's hard, but you can get a lot out of such workouts.

First we would do a 20-minute warm-up. Then we would do a four-and-a-half-minute big gear effort, say, pedaling at 80 rpm and a heart rate of 180 beats per minute. This would simulate a big climbing effort, and we would even sprint all-out for the last 30 seconds. Then without stopping, we would immediately do 15 minutes pedaling at 100 rpm. Together that would be a 20-minute sequence, and we would do the same effort six times for a two-hour interval workout.

That was a good workout to simulate attacking on a climb, because often attacks come at the end of a climb. So by sprinting all-out for the last 30 seconds at the end of the sustained effort, we were essentially mimicking attacking while climbing and sprinting over the top of a climb.

Another workout I liked was repeat one-kilometer intervals. An all-out one-kilometer effort is important in bicycle racing, especially for a breakaway rider like me, because you often need to put in really intense one-minute efforts to make a breakaway. So we would do 10 one-kilometer efforts. We would ride one kilometer all-out with full recovery to better prepare our bodies for a full-out intense kilometer effort.

With Denis, I also did a lot more motor pacing; you know, riding behind a scooter or motorcycle. I never did enough of that before, and it's so important, because it really allows you to train at race speed and forces you to spin your legs while pushing a bigger gear, which you do all the time when racing in the pack. And we would do intervals by basically attacking the scooter, which was just like attacking the pack. Such efforts are essential, because once the scooter catches up, you must be able to recover while riding behind the scooter, which is going at race speed.

At GAN, which became the Crédit Agricole team in 1999, we really focused on intensity. In training, I rode a lot fewer total kilometers, but I did a lot more hard efforts. I honestly don't know if there was a day when we didn't do something intense. One day we would do medium intervals, and on another day more speed-related intervals, but pretty much every day—unless it was a real rest day—we did intervals.

Diet also became more and more of a focus once I joined the GAN and Crédit Agricole teams. When I first started with GAN in 1998, there were still *les baguettes et vin rouge* on the dinner table at night. But in the years that followed, we replaced the white bread with whole-grain bread, and wine just sort of slowly disappeared, as cyclists looked increasingly to eliminate wasted calories. It's funny to look back, though, because in the beginning, it was perfectly normal to have a bottle or a carafe of wine at the team table with dinner. One of the advantages to allowing wine was that there was no abuse, because it wasn't a taboo in any way, shape, or form. But at the end of the day, wine still represents empty calories for a cyclist, and counting calories became more and more important to me as I matured as a professional.

My training continued to evolve when I went to CSC in 2004. CSC was a very forward-thinking team, but the change in training wasn't radical.

One thing was that there was more of a difference between hard days and rest days. Hard days could be even more intense than they were at Crédit Agricole, but rest days were really that, real rest. With Crédit Agricole, we might do a three-hour ride on a rest day with some light intensity. But with CSC we might actually take the day totally off.

Still, the hard days could be really hard, and it wasn't uncommon for us to mix a six-hour day with intervals. In the middle of that, we might have some 20-minute medium-intensity intervals followed by some climbs with sprints. We could alternate between different levels of intensity within a long ride. A normal day of training with Bjarne would generally have an hour or an hour-and-a-half of intervals. Again, we would train in three-day blocks—not unlike the old East German days—but in a very different fashion. On the first day, for example, we would concentrate on medium-intensity intervals. The next day, we would do more speed work, and the third day would be harder again.

With Crédit Agricole we didn't have the SRM power-meter technology, where we trained according to watts and power output. Instead, most of our training was based on our heart rates.

Bjarne was one of the first guys to really use the SRM system, and he had us all training according to our watts. Today everyone does that. It's the status quo. But back in the day, plenty of riders and teams did not yet organize their training around power output. As a result, our training became more individualized. While we would often start out training together, everybody just went at their own pace according to their heart rates, speed, and power outputs once we started the intervals.

A typical first day might include a series of 40/20s, for example. Basically, a 40/20 is when you push a big gear at 80 rpm on a climb for 40 seconds, followed by 20 seconds of spinning the smallest possible gear. Big guys like me might push around 450 watts during one of these intervals.

The second day might be a speed day, when we would do four 20-minute team time trials, with our pedal cadence hovering around 110 rpm.

On the last day, there would often be big-gear intervals. One of Bjarne's favorites would be these intervals where we would do five minutes sitting and then five minutes standing, while pushing a big gear the whole time.

One thing that was really different, however, was that in between intervals, we would really go easy, whereas on Crédit Agricole, we would still move along at a good pace. But Bjarne would say, "No, no, this is about the intervals! Don't kill yourself in between." That said, the overall training was simply harder with Bjarne than it was in the Crédit Agricole days. There was more quantity and more intense quality work. We did a lot of training camps in Italy, where Bjarne was living at the time, and honestly, there were times when I was just ready to buy a ticket and go home. There were moments when I actually said to Bjarne, "Bjarne, I'm just fucked. I can't keep going, let alone recover to be ready for the next race!"

Bjarne would just look at me and say, "Trust me. I've done this before. I can tell when you're tired enough!" And I've got to say, he was generally right in that regard. Heck, my first year with Bjarne, we actually finished one, two, three in the Tour of the Mediterranean, a big early-season French race. That was pretty impressive and provided me with an immediate demonstration of the value of Bjarne's approach.

Looking back, I would say that Bjarne's approach was just too hard for the young riders. Every year I saw neo-pros come to the team, and they were always really motivated. They wanted to show themselves, to prove themselves. They would come to the early-season training camps and do all the intervals full gas, but then you wouldn't see them for two months afterward. And when they would show up at the races, they were just dead.

For older, more mature riders like me, however, Bjarne's system was perfect.

There was a lot of thinking and planning behind the training programs. And then, of course, when it came to diet and equipment, Bjarne was really ahead of his time.

With CSC, we always had our time trial bikes set up and ready to go at the first training camp early in the year. And in those camps, we always had split days with two rides. We would ride on our TT bikes for two or three hours just to get used to riding in a time trial position for extended periods. You know, it's funny. Even late in my career, I still would see teams putting their time trial bikes together the night before Paris-Nice in March. That just killed me! I'd be like, "Are you kidding me? Are you really that stupid? You're just going to give up five or ten seconds like that because you're not prepared on the tech side?" Heck, Paris-Nice is often won by five or ten seconds! It never ceased to amaze me how unprofessional some professional teams could be.

Today, a lot of teams have become more sophisticated with their training and technical development, but Bjarne was definitely one of the first.

And after some teams began catching up to us in terms of technology and equipment, Bjarne really started to focus on food and diet. In the beginning, we had plenty of cookies and goodies. But after three or four years, we really focused on eating right. Specialists came in and lectured us on fats, for example, and how the body breaks those down. And we were one of the first teams to have a truck with our own kitchen that would follow us around to races, cooking healthy meals.

For a few years, all this attention to detail, be it in training, diet, or equipment, gave us a huge advantage on the road. Afterward, other teams took the same approach, such as the Highroad/HTC team and Team Sky after that. But you can only benefit from marginal gains like that for a couple of years before other teams catch up to you.

At the end of the day, the circle is round. You can shape it into an ellipse for a moment, but it is round. A bicycle has two wheels. You're not going to completely rework the idea. But Bjarne was always looking for an edge. He used to say, "Training hard is easy. Training smart is the hard part!"

To be honest, I was never consumed entirely by such fine points. Perhaps that's one reason I never won the Tour de France. Perhaps I wasn't consumed enough with the endless details. That's a choice you have to make as a cyclist. Perhaps the guys who win the Tour de France are the guys who are capable of taking everything they do to the point of perfection. But if you dedicate yourself to achieving perfection, you probably won't have time to go fishing. You'll never have time to go for an ice cream because, well, ice cream is poison for you. You'll never have time to go to the swimming pool with the kids, because sitting in the sun isn't good for you, or the chlorine isn't good for you.

I just could never think 24 hours a day about training, stretching, core-muscle training, and diet. I loved cycling and was dedicated to my profession, but it was always important for me to have a life, as well. And if that meant I needed to sacrifice 1 or 2 percent, then I was willing to do that to gain some quality and balance in my life. I was already a father by the time I turned professional. Family was always important to me. Cycling was not my only priority. I also wanted to be a good dad, a good friend, and a good husband and to give the people I loved a place in my life. Also, I come from the country. I come from a simple life, and I always wanted to keep life as simple as possible. Start out simple, because life will get complicated enough by itself.

I was also fortunate that I had a pretty high metabolism and never had to struggle to make weight like some riders do. As the years went by, with all the kilometers in my legs, well, weight just wasn't an issue. And a lot of those kilometers were spent on the front. Let me tell you, when you're riding tempo on the front for your team, or when you're in a breakaway, you're burning a lot more calories than when you're sitting in the pack looking pretty.

Fortunately, I didn't have to spend a lot of time focusing on the details. I always trained hard, and that was always enough for me to show up at races and be competitive without worrying about every single watt I was producing. To me, it always came naturally. I was lucky in that regard, because I just couldn't obsess over details.

You know, I do have an SRM system on my bike. It even has my name on it. But for years, I actually refused to use an SRM in races because I just didn't want a computer telling me that I was about to explode in 20 seconds. If you're an experienced bike racer, you already know that!

By the time I moved to Team Leopard in 2011, I was definitely more in the maintenance mode. I mean, when you reach 36, 37, you're not going to improve. At that point in your career, if you can just stay at the same level, it's a success. In fact, later in my career, I was sometimes lazy about sending my data to the coaches. But as long as I showed up ready to race, everyone was happy. Team trainers have to follow 24 or 25 riders at one time. So if they don't have to worry about a guy like me, then that just makes their job easier.

SACRIFICE

"I am not accepting defeat here.
I do not accept this!"

Jens as seen by Stuart O'Grady (teammate on GAN, Crédit Agricole, and CSC):

Jens was nothing if not the ultimate teammate. I'll never forget the first time we met him at a training camp. He showed up with the funny haircut and his funny accent and, all of a sudden, started throwing out these Australian expressions he'd learned from racing down under. We hit it off immediately!

Soon enough, he moved down to Toulouse to be closer to the boys, and he fit right in. We trained hard and we barbecued hard. We would go out and just smash ourselves on the bike. Back then, training was not so focused on specific intervals and stuff. We just went out and, BANG, someone would attack. It was basically a full-on race every day, but just among ourselves. And right away, you could see that he just had this massive engine.

Bloody hell! With Jens, there are just so many stories, because he was always there when you needed him. I don't know how many times our job would be to cover the early breakaways in a race, and he was always there. He was just relentless! When you're covering the early breaks, you have to follow all the attacks. Sometimes I would just need a break to recover. But when I would look up, Jens was still going! I swear he was attacking his own shadow sometimes! You just couldn't stop him!

Perhaps our best moment came in the 2001 Tour de France when I had the yellow jersey, and then Jens got in a breakaway and took it himself. I was just so happy! There wasn't anyone else in the whole peloton that I would have preferred to pass it to than Jens. He just gives to everyone. He gives so much out, so I was so happy be able to give something back to him.

In some ways, our careers were very similar. We both left Crédit Agricole the same year, and then in 2006, we joined up again at CSC. By that point in our careers, our roles started to change, and the team would often need us to simply ride tempo on the front to protect the interests of one of our team leaders. And again it was often Jens and me. We bonded even more then. I don't know how many kilometers we shared at the front, but it was astronomical! We made a pretty cool team.

So when I say that he was the ultimate teammate, he really was, because, well, you could just rely on him every day from January until October.

I HAD A LOT OF GREAT TIMES HELPING MY TEAMMATES WIN RACES, BUT PROBABLY MY GREATEST MOMENT ON THE CSC TEAM CAME WHEN MY BUDDY BOBBY JULICH WON THE PARIS-NICE RACE IN 2005. I'll never forget going into the final stage in Nice. I had the green points jersey, and Bobby had the yellow jersey. But we didn't have any teammates left in the final kilometers of the final stage.

Now the final stage of Paris-Nice almost always finishes on the Col d'Eze, this mythical climb outside Nice. Some years we finished with an uphill time trial, but in other years, like in 2005, it was the final climb of the race. And since the race is often decided by seconds, everybody knows this is the last chance to turn the tables. So there we were, going up the Col d'Eze. We knew we were going to be attacked heavily, but there was nobody there to help us out!

First Franco Pellizotti attacked, then Davide Rebellin attacked, then Alejandro Valverde attacked. Then, anybody who had anything left at all after a week of racing attacked. Pretty soon guys were going on all sides. It was crazy! But I swore to myself that I wasn't going to let anything happen to my friend Bobby! I was the last man between disaster and glory. And I just said, "Bobby, I'm not going to let anything happen so that you lose the jersey on the last day! It's just not going to happen! We're not going to let any of them get away. I'm going to bring each one of them back one by one!" And that's what I did. It was just one of those moments when I said, "I am not accepting defeat here. I do not accept this! Not for Bobby!"

Bobby sacrificed himself many times for me and my success, and I was determined to make it happen for him. This was going to be *his* day. It was my moment to show loyalty and friendship to him, and I knew that his wife, Angela, and his daughter would be there at the finish line. Ending up on the podium together with Bobby and seeing the tears and happiness in the eyes of his family made it all worthwhile. I have been asked many times about my best moment on the bike, and if I really have to pin it down to only one single moment, it would probably be this day. Simply it was so good to see my friend winning, and knowing that I gave it all I had to make his dream come true was really rewarding. Later, when Bobby and I talked, we both agreed that if I had wanted to, I could have attacked myself and taken the stage win and the overall win myself, but that made our moment together even better. It was clear that I did it for our friendship and not for selfish reasons. Needless to say we are friends forever.

For me, winning Paris-Nice that year was right up there with winning the Tour de France with Carlos Sastre in 2008, which for any cyclist is pretty much a dream come true.

I'll never forget that Tour. We were so strong that year. Not only did we have Carlos but also we had Frank and Andy Schleck, not to mention Fabian Cancellara. Honestly, I think our worst rider on the team, our weakest link that year, was a Tour de France stage winner. We were just so strong that year that it felt like riders were afraid to attack us. That's the kind of depth we had. We had the power of numbers working for us. And we made good use of it! We intimidated the competition and shut down the breaks whenever we wanted. Oh, those were the days when cycling was just easy and fun!

But, obviously, cycling is rarely easy and fun. During my years at CSC, we were often considered the best team in the world. Yet winning the Tour de France was another story. While we often placed well, victory was elusive. That all changed in 2008, of course.

From the beginning of the season, Carlos Sastre was our designated leader for the Tour. Carlos had finished fourth the year before, and we really thought he had a chance to win. The first time trial was short, so we knew he wouldn't lose too much time early on, and then he would really be able to go on the attack once the race hit the mountains.

But Frank and Andy Schleck were coming on strong, too. Frank, in particular, was just racing brilliantly. He pulled to within a second of the Australian rider, Cadel Evans, who wore the yellow jersey on the last day in the Pyrénées. Then Frank grabbed the jersey on the first stage of the Alps.

I'll never forget the stage that finished up the Hautacam climb in the Pyrénées. We had great tactics, and we had the legs to carry them out. As a result, we just blew the race apart, and a lot of our rivals lost time to us.

The race went over several key climbs before the finish, including the legendary Tourmalet Pass. As planned, Fabian Cancellara got in the early breakaway so that he could be in a good position and wait for us once we got over the Tourmalet. And I have to say, I was having one of the best days of my life. My job was to set a strong tempo on the

Tourmalet to put pressure on challengers. I knew I had Frankie, Andy, and Carlos on my wheel, and my job was to drive the pace as hard as possible with them tucked right behind me.

Those days, when I was able to really turn myself inside out for the team, for my friends, go down as some of the greatest moments of my life. I was just enormously proud! And when it happens on a climb like the Tourmalet in a race like the Tour de France, wow, it doesn't get better!

The adrenaline rush is incredible! You're swarmed by fans all around, yelling at the top of their lungs. Hands are reaching in from all sides. There's just a police motorcycle in front of you, opening this sea of people. Yet all this time, you have to be focused on your job, on taking your teammates up the climb smoothly. You have to come out of each turn smoothly and not accelerate until your teammates have also exited each turn. You're sort of in a tunnel, driving the race, but the race is the Tour de France. And you know your teammates won't forget it. These are just goose-bump moments that you will remember forever. You know that in the preseason training camps the following year, people will look back and remember those rides.

Once I hit the summit, I knew big challengers like Spain's Alejandro Valverde had already been dropped, so I went as hard as I could down the descent until we caught Fabian Cancellara, who seemingly just went even harder. Down into the valley and up again at the start of the final climb, we were just driving it. At one point, Bjarne even came on the radio and said, "Ah, Jens, are you okay? There's still a fair amount of racing left."

And I was like, "No, I'm good here. Trust me!"

That day couldn't have worked out any better. Guys like Valverde were suddenly out of contention, and Cadel was our biggest challenger. But after the Pyrénées, Cadel didn't know if he should focus on Carlos or Frank. It was just a brilliant team ride.

Once Frankie took over the yellow jersey in Prato Nevoso, a lot of people probably thought we were going to ride for him from that point on. And a lot of teams probably would have done just that. But I think that's where we really showed team unity and savvy.

No stage illustrated that more than the final mountain stage up the Alpe d'Huez. Frank had won the same stage just two years earlier. And as I said, he was going into it this year with the yellow jersey on his back.

He could easily have said, "Guys, this is my chance, and I deserve it. I deserve your full support now." But that's not at all what happened. Instead, both Frank and Andy said, "No, the plan was always to ride for Carlos, and we should still ride for Carlos." Andy, who was probably the strongest on that day up Alpe d'Huez, said, "Hey, I'm still young. I have more Tours to come."

And Frankie said, "Yes, I know I'm in the lead now. But I only have 40 seconds on Cadel. And we still have a time trial to come. That's not much. I might hold on to the jersey today, but it will be hard for me to keep it in the final time trial. Our best chance is to make the race hard as hell today. We need to sprint full gas into the bottom of the Alpe d'Huez, and then Carlos just has to explode, BANG, up the climb and take as much time as possible out of Cadel. He's a better time trialer than me and has a better chance to win the race."

In all my years of cycling, the Schlecks demonstrated one of the greatest examples of sportsmanship I've ever seen in that race. What better example of team spirit can you have than Frankie sacrificing his yellow jersey for a teammate? Without the team, Carlos would have had trouble gaining so much time. But with Frank and Andy controlling the race, it was very hard for anyone to chase. And even if someone like Cadel had chased after Carlos, he would have had to contend with Frank and Andy sitting on his wheel, saving themselves for a big counterattack. Basically, we cornered Cadel. But you can only employ such tactics when you have a really strong team.

From the beginning of the season, we just had a game plan and we never varied from it. Bjarne had total confidence in Carlos and put no pressure on him to get results earlier in the year. Heck, I remember in the Critérium du Dauphiné-Libéré, the big warm-up race for the Tour, Carlos wasn't even in the top 20. A lot of people—even some of us on the team—wondered if he was really going to be a contender in the Tour. But Bjarne was unwavering. And as he so often was, Bjarne was right!

That was just an amazing year for us. Carlos not only won the Tour but we also won the team classification. And the day we finally rolled into Paris all together was a dream come true. Like I said, being part of a winning Tour de France team is a dream for just about any professional cyclist, and it sure was for me. I just really wanted to live that experience once. There's nothing like cruising into Paris, escorting the yellow jersey down past the River Seine under the summer sun and on up the Champs-Élysées.

To make matters even better, that year was one of the rare occasions when we finished as an entire team in Paris, so we were all there to savor victory. I'll never forget climbing up on the podium with Carlos in the middle of us and looking back and seeing the Arc de Triomphe. I remember saying to some of my teammates there and then, "Hey, maybe we should all just retire right here and now! Cycling will never be better than this!" And still today, it goes down as one of the top three memories of my career.

Perhaps we really should have retired. Only weeks later, Carlos announced he was leaving us to ride for the Cervélo team the following year. I think he just feared that the Schlecks were getting stronger and stronger and there simply would be too many leaders for any one team. But it was a shame, because it broke up perhaps the greatest single team I was ever on.

The Tour of Germany in 2006: My first win there, Look at my face—I really gave it my all. I could hardly raise my arm to celebrate my victory. (H. A. Roth)

TOUR OF GERMANY

"I won because I just wanted it more."

MY ROLE AT CSC CHANGED SIGNIFICANTLY FROM WHAT IT WAS IN THE CRÉDIT AGRICOLE DAYS. Although I had a lot of support to race for myself throughout the year, when it came to the Tour de France, I was really there to ride for my team leaders. As a result, a lot of bike racing fans didn't see me doing the "Jensie" thing and going out in breakaways like I had so often in years past.

But at CSC, I actually had some of my greatest personal wins, too. And two of them came in my own national tour, the Tour of Germany. After the days of the Peace Race, the Tour of Germany was my country's biggest stage race. Personally, I loved riding in front of my home crowd, but because I was always riding for foreign teams, I didn't have a lot of opportunities. The Tour of Germany, however, gave me a great opportunity, and I was always supermotivated to compete in it.

It may come as a surprise, because my career has been so international, but I am very proud to be German. Even though I spent my entire career riding on foreign teams, I always considered Germany my home. And even though I really enjoyed my six years living with the boys in Toulouse, there was never a doubt in my mind that I would eventually return to Germany and settle down there. After all, you are what you are. And not many people can just pick up, leave everything behind, and live the rest of their lives in another country.

That pride corresponds with my love for the Tour of Germany. Now, early in my career, the Tour of Germany came before the Tour de France, but midway through, they moved it to just after the Tour. That changed things for me because, generally speaking, I usually came out of the Tour in really great condition. So when I was at CSC, Bjarne said, "Look, Jens, considering how strong you are in the Tour, I think you could really do something in the Tour of Germany." Bjarne was one of those directors who could really give you confidence. And he was capable of finding qualities in riders that the riders themselves couldn't even imagine.

Traditionally, after the Tour, there are a bunch of criteriums, sort of like exhibition races for the stars of the Tour. They pay a start fee, so there's good money to be made. But you can get sucked into a downward spiral if you do too many of them, because they're exhausting. And at the end of the day, the results don't even matter because they don't carry any points on the International Cycling Union calendar.

So, in 2006, I decided that instead of wasting a lot of my energy on these criterium races, I would just do a couple of them to keep my body used to the rhythm of racing. That allowed me to focus mostly on maintaining my condition through the Tour of Germany.

I'll never forget that race. Right after the Tour, I flew to Dortmund, where Egon, my dad, picked me up. I had one criterium in Ratingen, a town near Dortmund, on Monday, and one the next night, too. But otherwise, I did some easy rides for the rest of the week and watched my diet so I could stay as close to my Tour de France race weight as possible.

My dad stayed the whole week with me. He did all the driving and guarded my spare wheels during this criterium while I was out training.

Some days he went grocery shopping, cleaned my bike, and washed my car. He told me to not stay too long at the sponsor parties and to only drink *Apfelschorle,* a really common drink in Germany that is half apple juice and half sparkling water. He was really taking care of me and supporting me in every way. On a rest day he kept me company, visiting the Cologne Zoo. He was my mate for the whole week and the key part to my success the following week during the Tour of Germany.

The Tour of Germany started the next weekend. The first day was a rainy road stage. I lost about 10 seconds but was still close to the leaders. Then, a couple of days, later I got in a three-man break in the final kilometers and won the stage.

I had studied the final kilometers in the road book before the stage and knew it finished on a sort of bike path, so if I came out of the last corner first, it would be very hard to pass me before the finish. That's exactly what I did, and it worked out perfectly, because I won the stage and moved into third or fourth place. A couple of days later, we had our first mountaintop finish. Levi Leipheimer, an American on the German Gerolsteiner team, won the stage, but I managed to finish in the top five that day and move into the race lead.

The next day was the queen climbing stage, finishing up on top of the Arlberg Pass in Austria. That was a very hard finish for me because, as you know, I'm not a pure climber. I got a bit lucky that year because the race organizers canceled the next-to-last climb because of snow, so I just had to focus on making it up that one big climb at the end. On the final climb, I got dropped. But I knew that the road leveled off near the top when we went through a tunnel. So I knew that I had a really good chance to catch back up. While it's a known fact that I am not a natural born climber, maybe not too many know that I am pretty good at false, flat mountains. Since it flattened out a little at the top of that mountain, I knew as soon as I could go back into the big chain ring, I was going to be good. No little 65 kg climber was going to beat me there.

And that's exactly what happened. Instead of going into the red just to hold on to the leaders, I limited my losses and dropped back on the steepest section. But then I really attacked once the road flattened out. I finally caught the leaders in the last 500 meters. And I could see that they were just demoralized to see me return. I just kept on going and ended up winning the sprint. I could barely raise one arm in victory, and two meters beyond the line, I was at a complete standstill. That's how wasted I was. But my performance was good enough to lock up my first victory in the Tour of Germany.

On German TV, the commentator Ulli Jantsch quipped, "The last time I saw a comeback like that was in *Ben-Hur*!"

The only problem was that there was some skepticism about my win, because the Tour of Germany came on the heels of a scandal-ridden 2006 Tour de France. The Tour started with Operation Puerto and saw Germany's biggest star, Jan Ullrich, kicked out of the race even before it started, as well as my teammate Ivan Basso and the entire Liberty Seguros team. And then, let's not forget, the winner, Floyd Landis, failed a drug test only days after the Tour, just days before the start of the Tour of Germany.

The press was really split. Some really celebrated my victory. But some of the media were skeptical that a big rider like me, someone who isn't a really strong climber, could win the Tour of Germany. But I had finished 48th in the Tour de France, and only 2 of the 47 riders who finished in front of me were at the start of the Tour of Germany. I was supermotivated not only because it was my national tour but also because I lived like a monk the week after the Tour de France to stay focused. So I knew how I had won.

Unfortunately, things only got worse the following year, because everyone was so burned out after learning all the details of Operation Puerto and the Landis affair. Nonetheless, I returned to the Tour of Germany as the defending champion. Now my win the first year may have come as a surprise to some, but when I came back the next year, everybody knew I was there to win. Fortunately for me, there was a team time trial early in the race, something my team was always good at.

On the very first stage, I surprised everybody when I grabbed a bonus second at the bonus sprint midway through the stage. It was a flat stage, and everybody knew it would be a field sprint. But nobody expected me to attack at the intermediate sprint. Yet that's what I did! A kilometer away I just launched. Everybody was looking at me like, "What the fuck, Jens!" But I got that single extra bonus second, which came in handy in the team time trial the next day.

Because the first stage was a sprint stage, nearly everybody would go into the time trial with the same time. But that one little second moved us up in the team classification and allowed us to start later in the team time trial (TTT), which is always a big advantage because it allows you to gauge your times on the time splits all the other teams clocked when they left earlier. So you see, I may have looked stupid going for that measly bonus second, but there was real method to my madness.

And then, of course, we had another huge advantage going into the team time trial—Fabian Cancellara. Fabian was simply the world's best time trialist in 2007, so you can only imagine the advantage that gave us in a team time trial.

It was so impressive riding behind Fabian when he was in good shape.

I still have this vision of going downhill behind him on the TTT. Fabian was leading, and we were doing 75 kilometers an hour down this hill! The only problem was that Fabian was doing 80 kilometers an hour and we were losing ground to him. I just kept thinking, "I can't go any faster! I don't want to go any faster! I'm scared shitless!" This TTT wasn't on a highway or anything. No, we were on some small roads. And in case you didn't know, time trial bikes don't handle as well as normal road bikes to begin with. So when I say I was scared shitless, I was really scared! I was behind Fabian, and I lost about 50 meters by the time we got to the bottom of the hill. But the guys behind me lost 50 meters on *me*, so we were going crazy fast. And then at the finish, Fabian took this massive pull with 3 kilometers to go until the final 600 meters. He was just spinning along at 60 kilometers an hour. We were going at warp speed! I remember that whole time just saying to myself, "Please don't pull off, Fabian! Please don't pull off!" I knew I'd never be able to pull through and keep that speed.

But, in the end, we kept things together enough to win the time trial and, thanks to my little bonus second from the day before, I took over the race lead.

Now, of course, there was still a lot of racing ahead of us, and one stage included this supersteep Rettenbachferner climb. I'll never forget that climb, because on that day, I used the smallest gear ever in my career, a 38 x 28! But that was my only chance to get to the top with any chance of winning the overall race.

What I didn't know going into the stage was that, on this day, I would receive two amazing, unexpected gifts. The first came from the race organizers, who, fortunately for me, did not plan for other climbs on the stage (so as in the year before, I could just focus on the final climb).

Then I got a gift from Levi Leipheimer, who was now riding for the Discovery Channel team. Basically, they did all the work all day long. From the start of the stage, Discovery just went to the front and rode tempo all day. Now I'm in the yellow jersey with CSC. We're not exactly a shabby team. But Discovery didn't ask for any help. Obviously, Levi wanted to win the stage and take the jersey over on that stage. But it worked out perfectly for us, as we were able to just sit and save our energy for the final climb.

When we finally hit the climb, Levi's teammates just blew up one after the other, POW, POW, POW!

Suddenly, after only four switchbacks, Levi's team was gone, but I still had with me my teammate, Chris Anker Sørensen, a brilliant climber who can really hurt himself. Suddenly, there were only 10 riders left.

Chris went to the front and just drilled it. And then I prepared to make what to this day I would call one of my greatest moves—the bluff! With Chris on the front, I took about 10 deep breaths and then rode up alongside him with my water bottle in my hand and said really loudly, so everyone could hear, "Hey, Chris, I think we're good here. We dropped just about everybody and I'm in yellow, so we can let the others do the work if they want. If they want to attack me, let them attack. We're good!" I was talking to Chris, but really, I was talking at Levi, making sure he could hear me.

So we eased up a little bit and a couple of guys did attack, but my main rivals like Levi or the Italian, Damiano Cunego, actually lost time.

At the end, I looked unbeatable, but as I said, with the recent wave of doping scandals, some were skeptical. The irony was that while I may have looked invincible, I was actually bluffing!

When I think back on my two victories in the Tour of Germany, I think I won because I just wanted it more. It was my national tour, so I was supermotivated, and as a result, I remained focused after the Tour de France and maintained my condition.

I, of course, was sensitive to the weight of suspicion. In 2006, Ivan Basso, my team leader, was suspended from the Tour, and Floyd Landis, the Tour winner, tested positive. And in the 2007 Tour, the big prerace favorite, Alexander Vinokourov, was expelled from the race for a positive test. At one point before the Tour of Germany in 2007, I even asked Kim Andersen, my team director, if it wouldn't just be better if I finished third or fourth. But Kim just said, "No, we don't race that way. If you have the legs to win, then win. We'll answer questions later. But we're not going to throw away a race because your head says no."

Cycling was getting so complicated that you would find yourself asking stupid questions like "If I can win, should I win?" It was just so confusing, pretty much for everyone.

At the end of 2007 T-Mobile, the biggest German team, removed their name from their team jersey. They honored their contract, and the team continued as Highroad, but T-Mobile no longer wanted to associate their brand with our sport. And the same thing happened with Lidl, the supermarket chain that was the title sponsor of the Tour of Germany. In 2007, the second year I won, they removed their logo from the yellow jersey and replaced it with a motto, "Stay Clean." And the Tour of Germany came to an end a year later, after the 2008 edition.

I'll never forget that, during the 2007 race, a television commentator said, "Well, we sure hope Jens Voigt can live up to the motto on his yellow jersey." I was just outraged. I thought, "How dare you throw shit on me for no reason just because you think everybody is in the same boat!" Things were bad!

It was about this time that I decided to stop being the rider representative for the CPA. I just didn't want to be a spokesperson for the sport anymore. I was getting criticized from all sides. If I spoke out against doping, somebody was bound to say, "Are you insane? Why don't you keep your mouth shut?" But then someone else would say, "Hey, why don't you say more?" I'm just too thin-skinned to handle that kind of responsibility. I'm too sensitive. It was hurting me, poisoning my soul. Constantly answering questions about doping was just killing me.

I was riding really well, too. I was perhaps even at the height of my career, but I hadn't had a good laugh in over a month. I was helpless to make people believe in me. There was so much guilt by association that I just wanted to handcuff myself to a journalist for three months. I figured that was the only way to really show that there was no doping going on. We would sleep in the same room. We would brush our teeth together, everything! I would not leave his eyesight for three months. And only then, after it was obvious that I still rode my bike as well as ever, could I gain some credibility.

And I did have my detractors. Some people didn't like me because I spoke my mind about doping and the importance of saying no. So many times, I would be at the dinner table at night and my teammates would say, "Hey, that was really good what you said. It's important that people understand that not everybody is doping." But then, the next day, somebody would ride up to me in the peloton and say, "Hey, why can't you just shut up?"

It was a tough period in cycling. It was impossible to take the sport at face value. That made it a tough time to be a cycling fan. And a tough time to be a rider.

CRASHING

"Hey! Why do you have to multiply the pain?
Can't you stitch one thing up after the other?"

Jens as seen by Chris Anker Sørensen (teammate with Voigt on CSC and Saxo Bank teams from 2007 to 2010):

I raced alongside Jens as a support rider for several Tours, but I will never forget his last Tour with the team in 2010. The race was in the Pyrénées, and Jens and I were assigned to cover the early attacks on the Col de Peyresourde. By the time we reached the summit, we were gapped just slightly, but then suddenly Jens crashed really hard.

Later, I heard that he was really banged up and that he managed to stay in the race by basically riding a junior-size bike for part of the stage. I could only imagine how exhausted he must be. We were rooming a lot that year in the Tour, and I was a bit nervous about what I would see when I got back to the room.

He was in the bathroom when I arrived, and all of a sudden I heard him scream, "Fuck! I can't take it anymore!" I figured that he must be in a whole lot of pain, but then he came out of the bathroom yelling, "And now I have a stupid sunburn on my back! It's too much!" I was speechless. His body was just filled with cuts and bruises, but Jens was mostly upset that—because the crash ripped his jersey open down his back—he now had a sunburn to contend with as well!

IF I HAD ONE WEAKNESS THROUGHOUT MY CAREER, IT WAS DESCENDING. And it resulted in two of my worst crashes. Early on in my career, I was okay with going down hills at 100 kilometers per hour with just a foam helmet on my head and a nylon jersey on my shoulders. I never dropped anybody, but I wasn't getting dropped, either. Yet over the years, I struggled to follow the speed of the downhills.

And as the crashes accumulated, my descending got worse. My worst crash without a doubt came in the 2009 Tour de France in the Alps. I have seen the pictures of me lying there on the road in a fetal position with blood streaming down from my head. Normally, that means a broken skull! And if I had landed a little differently that day, I could have ended up in a wheelchair or, even worse, I could have lost my life. It could have been really, really bad, with very little hope.

Still today, it remains one of my most painful memories and something I hate to discuss. If you only knew how many times I've had to talk about it, how many times I've had to relive it.

We were in the Alps on the final climb of the day, the Saint Bernard Pass, before dropping into Bourg Saint Maurice for the finish. Andy Schleck was in the white jersey and planned to attack Alberto Contador, who was in yellow. So at the beginning of the day, we came up with a game plan. It was one of those master plans, and we needed somebody to be in the early breakaway so he could drop back and help Andy when he attacked on the Saint Bernard. When Bjarne asked who wanted to commit to the early breakaway, he knew he only had to look at me once to get the answer he was looking for.

So that's what I did. I got in the early break. It wasn't easy. As a matter of fact, I remember thinking, "Gee, maybe I am getting older!" But I got in the break. And once I heard Andy was leading the attacks on the Saint Bernard, I dropped from the lead group and timed it so that the leaders caught me on this section where the climb leveled out a bit so I could help take some good pulls. When the group of favorites came up to me, there were Andy, Alberto Contador, and Bradley Wiggins left. Frankie was just a bit off the pace with Lance Armstrong, and after taking a good pull, Andy asked me to go back and pull Frankie back up. And that's exactly what I did. All of a sudden, I crested the summit with my two teammates. At that point, we were definitely in a good position, and I thought, "Hey, we could win this stage. If I ride good tempo on the front, we could catch the break and Andy or Frank could win the stage!"

That must have been seconds before I crashed. I was pulling at the front, and Bjarne came on the radio and said, "Hey, Jens, you don't have to do all the work here. Others can pull if they want to win the stage." So I pulled off to go back to the team car and get a few fresh bottles for the boys. And that was my last memory!

The next thing I remember was lying on my back, looking up at the ceiling of the ambulance. My first thought was, "How in the hell did I get here?" And then, of course, a half-second later, the pain set in. I was like, "Ouch! 1 + 1 = 2. Ambulance + pain = crash!" Then I realized that I couldn't move because they had me strapped down to prevent me from moving. And then things got blurry again, and I must have blacked out.

Now, each day on the Tour, the race organizers designate three hospitals, one near the start, one midway through the stage, and one near the finish. But when we got to the hospital, they took one look at me and said, "No! We're just a tiny country hospital. Get him a helicopter and get him to a major hospital."

The next thing I knew, I was being wheeled out of the hospital and toward a helicopter with its propellers already turning.

I next remember waking up on an operating table. A team of doctors was stitching together my left hand. Then, out of the corner of my eye, I noticed another team working on my face. And then I saw a third team disinfecting my right hand so they could stitch it together later. I just thought, "Hey! Why do you have to multiply the pain? Can't you stitch one thing up after the other?" That said, I was feeling no pain at that point, because I was loaded up with painkillers.

Then I went out again, and the next thing I remember is waking up in my hospital bed at about 10:30 that night. It was the first time since the crash that I was lucid in any way. I went back over the day and the collection of scattered memories of the race, the helicopter, and the operation. And then I told myself, "Okay, get yourself together!" And slowly, piece by piece, I started moving different body parts. First, I moved my left hand. "Okay, I can feel that." Then I moved the right hand. "Okay, I can move that." Then I was like, "Should I move my legs? Do I still have them?" I really didn't know. It was scary. I just didn't have any memory or knowledge of how much damage I had collected. Finally, I moved my leg. It was painful, but I moved it. And I could feel my toes. Then I forced myself to raise my arms. That hurt a lot, too. But at least after that very painful process, I understood that nothing was broken beyond repair. And from that point on, it was just a matter of time before I was back.

So then I thought, "Okay, I've got to call the family." So I pushed the button and called for a nurse to bring me a phone. I knew that the team had already called Stephanie, but I wanted to talk to her just to say, "Look, I'm okay!"

When I called her, I understood from what Stephanie was saying that the media was asking questions and reporting different things. As a matter of fact, some commentator even said, "It looks like Jens's chances to see the next morning are about 50-50!" So Stephanie was just in shock.

I said, "Listen, honey, it's going to be okay. I know your name, and I know we're married. I know we have five kids, and I know all their names and birthdays. I'm okay. I'm really badly damaged. But there's nothing that won't be okay. I just need time."

And then I started my long, slow journey back to competitive racing. Once I was back in Germany, I had appointments just about every day, healing and rehabilitating. But while the crash looked really bad, I came out of it pretty quickly.

Two weeks later, I was walking again. And if you can believe it, by the end of the season, I was lined up for the Tour of Missouri. I was committed to the idea that I was not going to let this crash, however bad it was, end my career. I really didn't want to be the rider who was remembered for ending his career in a bad crash.

Perhaps it was all those Jack London novels I read as a kid, but I always wanted to be in control of my own destiny. So many characters in his novels succeeded even when all the odds were seemingly against them.

Bjarne was really supportive and promised that I would have a contract the following year. So once again I was riding for Saxo Bank the following year. But, sometimes, history can repeat itself in some weird ways. Once again, I made the Tour de France team in 2010. And once again, a late-race crash in the mountains nearly brought my Tour to an end, just like it had a year before.

It was like déjà vu. This time, we were in the Pyrénées rather than the Alps. The stage started up a climb from the gun, straight up the Col de Peyresourde. I think we had six total climbs that day. Guys just went ballistic, attacking from the start, and the race was all broken up. I was just 15 to 20 seconds off pace at the top. I remember I was with my teammate Chris Anker Sørensen, and we set off in chase so we could catch the front group on the downhill.

Suddenly I heard BLAM! and my front tire blew out. I just had enough time to realize, "Oh, this is going to be painful." The next thing I knew, I was lying on the ground.

Just one year after my horrible crash, and there I was crashing on another mountain descent. And let me tell you, about the only part of my body that didn't hurt was my right ankle. The rest of me was all road rash. I was just lying there bleeding everywhere. When I finally got up, blood was spurting all over. I remember thinking, "This is like *The Texas Chainsaw Massacre*!"

But the worst thing of all was that I almost got forced out of the Tour for a second year in a row. The problem was that the first team car was behind Andy Schleck and the second had decided to go up ahead to hand out water bottles at the foot of the next climb. As a result, I had no spare bike. And my race bike was lying on the ground in pieces. I tried to call up on the radio to say, "Hey, boys, I need a bike!" But all I heard was the scratch of static.

The Tour medical staff wants to get me all bandaged up to stop the bleeding. So I'm sitting on the side of the road watching riders stream by me, one after the other, group after group. And I'm just thinking, "Oh, this doesn't look good!"

Then the broom wagon pulls up and asks if I want to get in. And I say, "OH NO! I DON'T NEED YOU! GET AWAY!" But there I am, with blood everywhere and no bike. I honestly started thinking, "Maybe I can steal a motorcycle from a cop! Maybe I can steal a horse!" Whatever, anything to get down that mountain to a team car and get a new bike!

Finally, the race organizers got me a bike. But it wasn't exactly what I was looking for. It was like this little yellow junior-size neutral support bike. It was way too small for me and even had old-fashioned toe clip pedals! But that was the only way I could get down the mountain. So I just took off flying down the hill on this little bitty bike! I had to ride it for about 15 to 20 kilometers until I finally got to a team car with my bike. And all I can say is that when I got on it, BOY DID I FEEL BIG!

Once I got down the mountain, I was able to reach Bjarne on race radio. He knew I was coming, so at a turn at the foot of the next climb, he found a cop and actually gave him one of my bikes, saying only, "This bike is for Jens Voigt. He's coming. Please give this to him!"

When I got to the same turn, I heard this voice yelling, "Monsieur Voigt, Monsieur Voigt!" And, finally, I got back on one of my bikes and still had a fighting chance to finish the stage.

But first, I had to catch up to the *grupetto*, that pack of stragglers that's just trying to stay on pace to make it to the finish before the time cutoff. And let me just say that desperate times call for desperate measures. I will admit that I got a few good, sticky water-bottle hand-ups. That's when a director hands out a water bottle and then you hold on to it real good while he accelerates for a moment. Each one of those gives you just a couple of highly valuable seconds to recover and regain some momentum. They're real lifesavers, and that was never more the case than on this day!

The first person I caught up to was the Australian sprinter Robbie McEwen. He was really struggling, and it looked like he might not make it to the finish. But I guess I looked a lot worse, because when he looked over and saw me, the first thing he said was, "MAN, YOU LOOK LIKE SHIT!" I mean, Robbie was fighting for his own survival and, by all accounts, looked pretty bad himself. But his only thought was just how bad I looked!

Even so, I was happy to hear that because, well, it meant that I was still alive. Robbie told me that another sprinter, Mark Cavendish, was up the road and that I should try and catch him, which I did. Mark Cavendish had three more teammates with him to make sure he survived the day and to help him through the stage: Mark Renshaw, Bernard Eisel, and Bert Grabsch, a strong German powerhouse. As soon as I reached them, they all repeated what Robbie had said, "MAN, YOU LOOK LIKE SHIT," which made me super happy. Then Bernie (Bernard Eisel) came to me and said "Listen, we're gonna go 'flatfuck' in the last descent, and I am sure you can't follow our speed on a descent after a crash like you just had. If you have any energy left, go ahead and gain some time on us and we will catch you later in the descent." That's what

I did and, fair enough, halfway through that descent, they came flying by. To this day, that was one of the biggest displays of sportsmanship I have seen in my career. They waited for me, slowing down and looking back over their shoulders to make sure I was still on their wheels. I mean, just to put this in perspective: There is Cav, a 2-million-dollar superstar of our sport, risking elimination from the biggest race in the world to slow down and wait for a beat-up, tired, hurting guy whom he probably didn't even know all that well. He and his teammates saved my day by making their own day harder. Because they knew and I knew that every second they slowed down meant more work on the flat to chase down that grupetto. And there was still another 100km to go and one major climb left in the stage. To make it even more impressive, there was no TV crew around to capture this display of fairness and camaraderie. The four riders just decided, okay, we can't let this guy down and leave him behind. Little stories like these are seldom told and make the beauty of sport, the beauty of cycling, to me. The surprising and unexpected moments of humanity among rivals is what, to me, is so precious about sports. Yes, fair and square, these four gentlemen saved my day. And now I can say "thank you, Mark, Bert, Cav, and Bernie."

Finally I caught up to the grupetto, and I just stayed there for the rest of the day. I think it's safe to say there has never been a moment when I was happier to be in the grupetto.

At one point, I started thinking of those books in the Discworld series by Terry Pratchett. In them, the protagonist, Cohen the Barbarian, is a 70-year-old guy who has survived everything imaginable. At one point, he and his band of old warriors capture a village, but then they find that they're surrounded by an army of thousands. And his only reaction is, "Oh man, it's going to take days to kill all these people!" And that's the way I was that day in the Pyrénées when I was lying on the ground. I was just like, "Oh no. I'm going to Paris this year, I'm going to Paris! There's just no way you're going to get me out of this race a second year in a row!"

ARMSTRONG

"There would be no Porsches and no Ferraris."

THE SPORT GOT HIT WITH ANOTHER HUGE DOPING SCANDAL IN 2012, WHEN LANCE ARMSTRONG WAS HANDED A LIFETIME BAN FROM CYCLING. I had already lived through some huge doping scandals with the Festina affair and Operation Puerto, but in many ways, the Armstrong revelations were even bigger. After all, Lance was the greatest rider, the biggest actor in cycling. He was the seven-time Tour de France winner and the Tour de France record holder, so when his own doping was revealed to the world, it had a huge effect on everybody in cycling.

Lance did so much to make the sport popular all over the world. But he did just as much to destroy it. It was almost like he single-handedly built it up only to break it down again. As the specifics came out, we discovered in detail how in-depth Armstrong's doping organization was, how bizarre it was, and how perfectly it had been executed throughout the team.

The negative impact was huge! Everybody involved in the sport had to answer questions about Lance and doping. Did you know something? Did you suspect something? If so, why didn't you say something about it before? It was stressful for everybody. It was like we were all guilty by association for many years. I had many questions myself. People were always asking me, "Jens, you raced in the same years. You were the same age. How could you not dope like Lance did? You must have known! You must have been part of it!"

It was exhausting. And after a while, after answering the same questions again and again, I was over it. I just kept telling people, "Look, I was a good, solid rider, but I never once had an over-the-top performance!"

I'm a good rider, period! I was good enough to get selected for the German sports school program, and as I said earlier, I was good enough to stay in the sports school year after year. You can only do that if you're talented. But I never won a Tour de France. I had some success, sure. And that's normal, because I'm talented and I work hard. But again, I never had any over-the-top performances. Nevertheless, the suspicion surrounding the sport made life hard for everyone in it. Lance was just such a big figure, the biggest in modern history, so it's normal that if he's caught taking performance-enhancing drugs, it's going to have a huge impact on everyone else involved in the sport, too.

Some journalists asked me if I felt cheated. I finished second to Lance in the 2004 Tour of Georgia, for example. So some people wondered if I felt like I'd been robbed of a victory. But as I've said before, I just don't think like that. I'm not going to poison my mind thinking about all the "what-ifs." I'm not going to think about every single race where I finished in second or third or fourth place behind riders who later tested positive for doping. That just doesn't make my life better or healthier. As a rider, you just can't continue if you're always thinking about getting beaten by dope cheats.

But thinking back on it now, yes, certain conclusions can be drawn. In that Tour of Georgia, for example, it took six days of racing and a really hard, steep uphill finish to Brasstown Bald in Georgia for me to lose 1 minute and 20 seconds to Lance. Two-and-a-half months later in the Tour de France, I was losing 10 to 15 minutes to him per day in the mountains, when I was really in peak condition. In those two-and-a-half months between the Tour of Georgia and the Tour de France, I trained hard. I was healthy and didn't crash. So where did the difference come? Was I doing something wrong? Or did something else come into play?

You have to remember, though, we're talking about 2004. Nobody knew what to think back then. There was suspicion around Lance, but there wasn't any proof yet! Don't forget, this is before Operation Puerto broke in 2006. This was before a lot of things came out that we didn't know about. In hindsight, yes, things are more obvious. I understand why suddenly I was, say, 25 percent less competitive than I had been only a couple of months prior. Today, equipped with the perspective afforded by history, we see things differently. But that was a good decade ago. We didn't know what we know today.

In addition, there are other factors that you can't ignore. A race like the Tour of Georgia has mostly rolling stages with maybe one hard climb. I can handle that. In the Tour de France, you have three or four hard mountains in a single day. That's just too much for me! I'm a big, powerful rider, but I'm not a pure climber. I'm just not. I can compensate with willpower and desire on one climb, perhaps, but not three or four climbs day in and day out. There are no secrets. You have to be a climber to excel at that kind of racing.

Also, you can't forget that my role in the Tour de France was different. I was not a leader. I was a support rider. I spent time and energy covering breakaways or chasing them down. I spent time and energy fetching water bottles for my teammates. I spent time and energy riding in the wind, protecting my team leaders. All those factors combine to explain why I lost so much time to guys like Lance in the Tour. Back then, I tried to focus on concrete reasons like those to explain the time gaps rather than speculate about doping. It's called survival. Sure, sometimes I was surprised that the gap between a rider like Lance and me suddenly increased so much. But I preferred to focus on tangible reasons for the differences.

Sometimes, we would speculate about a rider's performance at the dinner table with the team. We'd see a performance from a rider who had shown nothing for years and ask, "Where did that come from?" Or sometimes someone would go off training for a couple of months and come out and just go "bang!" Or as in my situation at the Tour of Georgia, I couldn't help but ask myself, "Hey, how did that happen? How could I almost be winning a big race against the best rider in the world and then, a couple of months later, just be a total shit kicker?"

To be clear, though, Lance didn't get in the way of my having a satisfying career. As we know, I rode for a long time. I made 17 starts in the Tour de France. Every time my contract expired, I would have offers from a fair number of teams. Most of the time, I was happy to stay where I was, and really I only competed for three different teams. GAN and Crédit Agricole were the same team, as were CSC and Saxo Bank, as were Leopard, Radio Shack, and Trek Factory Racing. Team names changed from time to time, but in terms of team structure, I only knew three. And that was fine with me. I liked the security.

There were times where I'd be out training by myself and thinking, "What could I do to get better?" But for me, I felt like I had a choice. Perhaps I could have become a big superstar by signing with certain teams and winning bigger races. But at the same time, I would have risked having everything blow up in my face. You know, after the Festina affair in 1998, it was still possible to ride clean and have a good career. The French teams were the first to take a strong position against doping, but other teams soon followed. And a lot of riders like me won smaller races or stages in the Tour without doping.

But somehow you just knew inside, or at least sensed, that if you were going to be a podium finisher in the Tour de France in that time, you would have to cross the line and do something illegal, that you would have to break the rules. And if you look at the Tour podiums in most of those years, that suspicion is pretty well confirmed, since just about every podium finisher in the Tour was involved in a doping scandal in one way or another. Either they tested positive at some point, they admitted to doping, or their names were cited in some very serious investigations.

And with certain teams, there just seemed to be a much greater chance that you would have to overstep the line and start doping. Yes, perhaps I could have won more big-time races if I had cheated, but my life would have been much more stressful. My career would have become this maddening cycle of lies and the constant fear of getting caught.

I always chose the other option, the one where you have a good solid career, a long career, but where there are no million-dollar contracts. There would be no Porsches and no Ferraris. I chose this option so that I could enjoy a safe and long career. For me, it was worth it, knowing that there were no skeletons hanging in my closet. But as a result, I never became a big superstar. I never won any really big races. Sometimes I do wonder what I could have accomplished with a little chemical help. With my talent and work ethic, maybe I could have been a podium contender. Instead, I think my highest Tour de France finish was when I placed 35th back in 2004. That said, I was always satisfied in knowing that I had achieved the maximum results possible with my natural talent and work ethic.

Perhaps my choice is a result of growing up in a Communist system. After the Wall came down, I had so many more opportunities than I ever thought possible. Heck, I was already living the life just being a professional cyclist! I already had been given so much more than I'd ever expected coming from my modest, small-town background, where my choices had been so much more limited. Sure, one can always dream about a bigger life. But I was always taught—and this goes back to my parents, Egon and Edith—that it wasn't right to take shortcuts to get somewhere if it was going to make someone else suffer. That's what doping was to me, a shortcut. And it was never an attractive option.

As a result, there were times when I refused to join certain teams because of their reputations. One of those teams was ONCE, a really powerful team in the 1990s, led by Manolo Saiz, who would later find himself at the heart of Operation Puerto. By that point, the title sponsor had changed to Liberty Seguros, but it was still the same team. On at least two occasions, Manolo made it clear that he would like to work with me. Now ONCE was one of the big teams. They had one of the first big team buses. At the time, I was with Crédit Agricole, and we just showed up to the start of a race in a camper. So there was a lot of glamour around ONCE.

But I was good at Crédit Agricole. I had good friends there and had fun racing there, so it never really happened. And in hindsight, it's safe to say that I'm happy that things worked out the way they did and that I stayed at Crédit Agricole.

And then there was US Postal, which asked me to join them not once but twice.

The Tour de France is many things. It's a great bike race. But it's also a huge job market. Those three weeks are when teams and riders do most of their talking and when many contracts get signed. At the Tour, you see the same people every day for three weeks. Before the start, team directors are often standing out by their team cars. So it's not uncommon that some will stop and chat with you. And often, conversations include talking about your contract and whether or not it's coming up at the end of the year.

With US Postal, I talked with Lance directly. Over the years, I'd chatted with him during races, when we were rolling out in the neutral zone before the official start or during a quiet moment in the race itself. Back in the day, there weren't many English speakers in the peloton. I thought it was great how Lance had come back from cancer, and we'd always chatted off and on. And then one day, he asked if I would be interested in joining him.

The first time came in 2000, when I was with Crédit Agricole. We had just finished the Pyrénées and were rolling along on a flat stage and Lance said, "Hey, man, why don't you come to our team? We could use you. We need a rider like you. You are a good rider, and we'd make you a better rider. We'd win some great races together."

But I just said, "Hey, I'm pretty happy where I am. Roger [Legeay] has always been good to me. It's a good team, and I have a lot of chances to ride for myself and explore my own limits."

I really liked the freedom I had on Crédit Agricole, and I knew that if I rode for Lance, I wouldn't have the same freedom. There was always a lot of suspicion and rumors around Lance regarding doping, which didn't attract me to the team. Nothing had been proven yet—far from it—but there was always suspicion.

And then there was another very big reason. US Postal just didn't seem like a fun team. They were so focused on winning that I was afraid I would just become part of a big machine. I always wanted to enjoy my team. So US Postal was never super-attractive to me.

Then, in 2003, Lance asked me again. This time it was a little different. It happened when the Tour de France was in the Pyrénées, after the mountaintop finish to Luz Ardiden. We were both called into doping control after the finish. Lance had won the stage and was wearing the yellow jersey, so he automatically had to do the drug testing. I finished in the grupetto that day, about 30 minutes behind. But I got called as part of the random testing that they do regularly at the races. Because Lance was wearing the yellow jersey, the Tour provided him with a helicopter evacuation off the mountain. That's standard procedure for the wearer of the yellow jersey, since he's always delayed for the podium and the doping controls. After finishing doping control, the race organizers offered me a seat in the official helicopter going down to Pau, where our hotel was. Getting off a mountain in the Pyrénées is never an easy thing to do in the Tour de France. The roads are smaller than in the Alps, and there are so many cars. I jumped at the occasion. So Lance and I started chatting going down in the helicopter, and he asked me again.

Later I learned that I was the only rider that Armstrong or US Postal had asked on two different occasions to join the team. I only learned that detail by circumstance, really. It was in the 2004 Tour of Georgia, when we were both fighting out the victory. One day, in a postrace press conference, a journalist asked Lance about his chances to win the race. And he looked over at me and said, "It depends on that man there." And then he went on to explain that I was the only rider he'd twice asked to join the team.

It was a funny moment. But I never regretted my decision, especially after all the news came out about the doping and after Lance finally admitted it.

You know, it may sound funny, but in some ways, I was surprised by how much of a shock Armstrong's admission finally provided. Evidence was mounting in the two years prior to his admission, and by the time he finally confessed, there was just an overwhelming amount of evidence against him. I mean, by the time he announced that he would talk to Oprah Winfrey, 90 percent of the people knew what it was going to be about. Yet, still, his admission was earth-shattering.

Lance was the greatest rider in modern history—such a high-profile figure—so it was just huge news all over the world. As I said, Lance was so big that when there was a problem for him, there was a problem for all of us. Though many of us hoped that the sport could just move on, it was impossible, because his admission reopened a lot of legal cases from the past, some of which are still ongoing today.

Lance paid a high price for his doping. You can argue about whether that price is too high or not, but he definitely paid a high price, because after years of lies and evasions, he missed the chance to have some negotiating power regarding his sentence. Many other riders who admitted guilt early and expressed contrition received reduced sentences. But Lance chose the path of denial and ended up painting himself into a corner. As a result, he also pissed a lot of people off, so when he finally did confess, he got the maximum sentence.

With every doping scandal, some people definitely pay a higher price than others. Look at Operation Puerto, for example. Initially, it was announced that up to 60 cyclists and 200 athletes from all sports, including tennis, soccer, and track and field, had been working with Dr. Fuentes, the man behind Puerto. But in the end, we only knew the names of maybe 10 cyclists maximum. No other names were ever revealed. That's an absolute scandal in this day and age! I mean, it was probably easier to find out who shot JFK than to find out who else visited and worked with Dr. Fuentes! That's just wrong! To sweep so many names under the rug in this day and age, wow. There must be some pretty big people, companies, or institutions involved.

So yes, Lance definitely paid the highest price in the US Postal doping affair. It's understandable. But also I feel it's time to move on from it. It's time to forgive. I mean, what are we going to do, shoot him to the moon? You know, I'll never forget a time in 2009 after my bad crash in the Tour de France. When I woke up the next morning in my hospital room after my surgery, I had a bunch of messages from my team, but only one other rider sent me a message. And that was Lance Armstrong. Obviously, he has caused a lot of damage, but he's not the devil, either.

Moments before starting the time trial in the 2011 Paris-Nice race. (James Startt)

LEOPARD TREK

"You can set the stage just perfectly. You can put all the pieces in place. But you cannot guarantee victory."

AFTER SIX YEARS WITH BJARNE RIIS, AN OPPORTUNITY AROSE IN 2011 TO JOIN A VERY EXCITING NEW TEAM, LEOPARD TREK. In many ways, it had the makings of a real dream team. In reality, the promise never materialized.

The team arose in Luxembourg through an initiative with Flavio Becca, our director Kim Andersen, and the Schleck brothers. In addition to that, it appeared that Bjarne was getting worn down from the constant search for sponsors and team stability. In 2008, CSC's sponsorship ended, and we started working with Saxo Bank. At first, we thought we would have a really great cosponsor with IT Factory.

But it quickly turned into a disaster. Right after the team survival camp at the end of the 2008 season, we visited the IT Factory headquarters in Denmark. It was strange from the beginning. We arrived at what was supposed to be a five-million-dollar sponsorship deal, and things were just so calm. The place was just not big enough or busy enough to support a cycling team because, well, a company that can afford a five-million-dollar sponsorship deal generally is going to be pretty active, with people visibly working. And that was not the case here. And the very next morning, news broke that the company CEO, Stein Bagger, had been on the run for three weeks with all kinds of money. Interpol had even launched a big manhunt for the head of what was supposed to be our new title sponsor!

It turned out that the IT Factory's factory never existed. The whole thing was an industrial Ponzi scheme! The company had apparently won awards for good business in Denmark, yet they never produced one thing!

The morning after our visit, when the news was just breaking, Bjarne pulled me aside along with Bobby and a couple of the older Danish riders and said, "Hey, boys, we have a problem. We don't have a sponsor!"

Fortunately, we had Saxo Bank as a sponsor, but it was a year-to-year deal and never very secure. As a result, it just seemed like Bjarne was getting worn down. He was spending so much time and energy looking for sponsors that he couldn't be as active in the team. He just seemed less connected to us. When I first started with Bjarne, he would be in the team car in early-season races such as the Tour Med until the last races of the year. But six years later, he wasn't in the car anymore at the Tour Med. He was a lot less present. It seemed like he'd lost the desire a bit. It seemed like he'd lost the passion.

I was still in the best years of my career, and my family on the road was Bobby Julich, the Schleck brothers, and Stuart O'Grady. So when the project in Luxembourg materialized and the Schleck brothers asked me to join them, there was no reason to hesitate. It was a no-brainer. One of my dreams toward the end of my career had been to help Andy win the Tour de France and to ride into Paris with him in yellow. To this day, that remains one of my regrets. Andy did eventually win a Tour when Alberto Contador was disqualified in 2010 (i.e., traces of

All smiles here, after grabbing the yellow leader's jersey for a second time in my career during the 2005 Tour de France. Joking in the post-race press conference I said, "I am confident I can defend the jersey tomorrow since it's a rest day!" And that's exactly what I did! (James Startt)

Climbing toward the Alpine summit in Courchavel wearing the yellow leader's jersey at the end of Stage 10 in the 2005 Tour de France. As you can see in the picture, I was moving at more of a crawl. It was a bittersweet moment. Still sick, I was eliminated from the race on the following day. (James Startt)

Lying on the road moments after my worst crash ever in the Tour de France on Stage 16 of the 2009 race. Apparently, I asked the doctor three times if I could continue. But to be honest I don't remember a thing from that moment. (James Startt)

Covered in bandages after crashing heavily on Stage 16, I was committed to finishing the 2010 Tour after crashing out in 2009. It was only after the finish in Paris, that I realized that I had two fractured ribs. (James Startt)

Another Tour, another crash, but this time there was no way I was stopping. There was just no way! (Robin Wilmot)

Here I am finishing with one-time teammate and long-time friend Thor Hushovd (right) in Thor's final day in the yellow jersey during the 2011 Tour de France. Thor and I first teamed up in 2000, and he was one of the best men at my wedding in 2003. (James Startt)

Inside the team bus as I prepare for Stage 14 of the 2013 Tour de France with my friend and teammate Andy Schleck. (James Startt)

Here I am racing through the center of Lyon during the opening time trial of my final Critérium du Dauphiné. Although I was in the final months of my career, I was already planning for the hour record attempt. (James Startt)

After struggling in the early season, I finally started to feel like myself in the 2014 Critérium du Dauphiné. Able to attack frequently gave me the confidence that I was prepared for one final Tour de France. (James Startt)

At the Trek Factory Racing team press conference at the start of 2014. Regardless of the season's outcome, I knew it would be my last. (James Startt)

I never really did like the cobblestones and I liked them even less in the rain. Here I am making the best of a bad situation Stage 5 of the Tour de France in 2014. (James Startt)

Getting the polka-dot jersey for best climber from Prince Harry after Stage 1 was a good way to kick off my final Tour de France in 2014. (James Startt)

To my incredible surprise the Tour de France gave me a yellow jersey for each of my children during my final Tour de France. They sprung this surprise on me in Mulhouse, where I won my first yellow jersey. Wow!

Seconds before going for the world hour record. Talk about being nervous! With my parents on hand and more than a million watching on television, I sure didn't want to finish my career as a loser! (James Startt)

In the closing laps I knew I would break the world hour record. Now it is just about withstanding the pain threshold. (James Startt)

Savoring my third and final victory in the Tour de France. (James Startt)

clenbuterol were found in his blood), but that's not same as riding into Paris with Andy in the yellow jersey on my wheel.

Andy was just a pure talent. You could see from the get-go that he had it! After all, he won the white jersey as the best young rider in 2008, 2009, and 2010, so it seemed like it was just a matter of time until he would win the race himself. He had more pure talent than even someone like Carlos Sastre. And because he was young, there was still so much potential for him to develop and get even better. When Carlos won the Tour, he was a mature rider at his peak. Andy was still improving. He seemed to possess the talent to become one of the great Tour de France riders of all time. So when the Schlecks asked me to join their team, it looked like a good fit. Bjarne could only offer me a one-year contract, while Leopard immediately offered me a two-year deal. For an aging rider like me, one that had five kids—and a sixth one on the way—the opportunity to ride for Leopard was too good to pass up.

During the Tour in 2010, Bjarne came to me and asked me very directly, "So, Jens, what's it going to be? Are you going to try the Luxembourg project or are you going to stay with me?" I told him that I wanted to try something new, and he understood. He tried to campaign a bit to keep me, but he knew that my mind was pretty much set. So he said, "Hey, no worries. I understand that after seven years, it's good to change. It's important to have new challenges."

Bjarne and I left on good terms, without a doubt, and we're still friends today.

But while Leopard Trek appeared to be the next superteam, things never really worked out that way. Why things didn't work out is still up for debate, but mostly I would say that it was for a combination of reasons.

First off, just based on points, with riders like such as Fabian Cancellara as well as Frank and Andy Schleck, we began the season as the top-ranked team in the world. I mean, before we pinned the first number on our backs at the first race, everyone was looking at us like we were the best. And I guess we believed it ourselves. As a matter of fact, I remember very well a meeting at the December training camp in which I said, "Hey, boys, I don't want to spoil the party or anything, but we're the number-one-ranked team in the world without taking one pedal stroke. That's the point. We haven't done it yet. We haven't earned that number-one ranking yet this year. We have a lot of expectations on us. We really need to focus. We can't afford to be lazy. We can't slack off. We need to perform the way people expect us to perform. It's always easier to reach the top than it is to stay on the top."

Looking back, I think people were too relaxed. The expectations were maybe too high, as well, but we were definitely too relaxed. I think it's fair to say that we were too cocky, too. There was a general feeling that we were going to be very good, that we were going to rule the world. I didn't want to be the bad guy and spoil the dream, but maybe with my age and experience, I should have stressed even more to the guys that we hadn't yet proven anything, that you have to work, because nothing comes easy in life. Perhaps I should have gotten in people's faces more and pulled the team back down to earth.

I think the whole team, all the way to the top, expected success to come easily. Our new team owner, Flavio Becca, expected that we would win left and right, that victory would just be a stroll in the park. But this is sports; victory is never easy. Look at any sport. Look at Formula 1 World Championships. Who would have expected that Sebastian Vettel would not win a fifth Formula 1 title after winning four years in a row? There is no guarantee of success in sports. You can set the stage just perfectly. You can put all the pieces in place. But you cannot guarantee victory.

In any sport, you're only as good as your last result. And we underestimated that age-old rule of sports at Leopard Trek.

We did do a lot of things right. The team was really well organized. Looking back over the years, I think we had one of the best-looking team kits. We looked great, and we were very, very well liked by the fans. I think that Leopard Trek team was the most popular team I've ever been on. We had the most applause of any team all the time, wherever we went. It was really impressive! It was just constant applause. So, in many ways, it was a dream project. It was a dream working on that team. And we had a lot of very good results. But they were mostly second- and third-place finishes. What we did not have were big victories.

Fabian Cancellara finished second in Milan–San Remo, and he finished third in the Tour of Flanders. I think it's safe to say that at Paris-Roubaix that year, he was the strongest rider in the race. He was the defending champion, and after his strong finishes in San Remo and Flanders, he was the heavy favorite. But there was a lot of negative racing that day. A lot of riders just seemed to be racing against Fabian. A big break got away, and Fabian pretty much had to chase them all down single-handedly. He caught just about everybody, but he couldn't catch the Belgian Johan Vansummeren, who soloed to victory, and Fabian finished second.

Fabian realized that it was going to be close to impossible to win that year, and in my opinion he decided "Okay, you wheel-suckers, I will decide who wins this race." And that's when he decided to let a no-name win, to punish all the self-declared prerace favorites for riding like little schoolboys and just chasing him down all the time instead of trying to win themselves. It looked like a whole lot of riders had the attitude of "We'll let anyone win except Fabian," and he decided to let the brave and courageous Johan Vansummeren ride away and win the race. You don't believe my theory? Well then, when was the last time an outsider won Roubaix?

Then in Liège-Bastogne-Liège, one of the hardest one-day classics, the Schleck brothers finished second and third. Two guys on the podium in a race like that is impressive, but it is not victory. That year, another Belgian, Philippe Gilbert, was having the best year of his life. He won all the Ardennes classics, the Amstel Gold Race, the Flèche Wallonne, and Liège. Nobody could beat him, including us, so we didn't manage to win any of the big spring classics.

Overall, we were the best team in the classics that year, since we had a rider on the podium in every one of the major races. But we didn't win one of them. Each time, Leopard Trek "only" finished second or third. That's what the press wrote, and that's what stuck in people's minds.

And then the same thing happened in the Tour de France, where Andy and Frank Schleck finished second and third behind Cadel Evans. How great is that, to have two brothers from the same team on the podium in the world's biggest bike race? But again, there was no victory. And because of the high expectations, the press, not to mention Becca, the team owner, were dissatisfied with our performance.

Flavio Becca was a real fan. He had a lot of theoretical knowledge of the sport. He knew the names of the teams and riders. At the first team camp, he already knew all the riders' names and most of the staff, as well. He was very enthusiastic, and he obviously put in an effort to look at team pictures and learn people's names. He wasn't just invested in the team, he was also committed to it.

But perhaps he saw it like a big investment or a game. Perhaps he saw a bicycle team as something where, if you invest so much money, you get so much in return. If you put in so many millions of dollars, then you get so many victories in return. Perhaps he felt that because he put in more money than a lot of other teams, he was going to get more victories. But sports aren't always like that.

A sport like cycling is all about giving maximum effort. One percent here and 1 percent there quickly adds up to 2, 3, 4, or 5 percent of a difference. And that's a lot. That's the difference between winning and losing. That's the difference between first and second place.

While Leopard Trek ultimately disappointed some, we still had a strong season and won the Tour of Lombardy, one of cycling's monuments, at the end of the season. That was a great victory by Oliver Zaugg, but it came too late. We never got the big win at the right time.

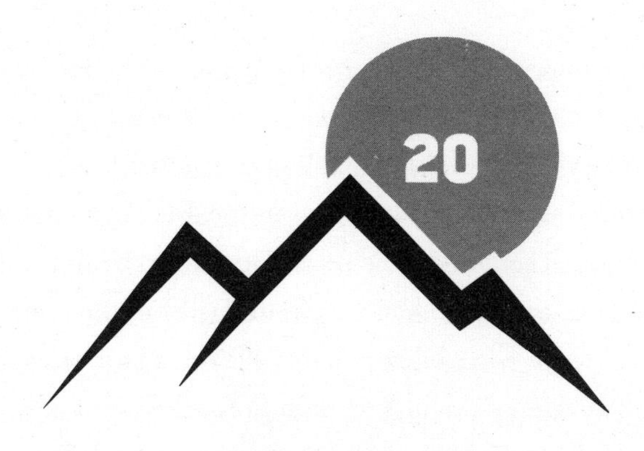

FAMILY

"I'm a grown-up man. I don't cry for victories, nothing. But I do cry when each kid arrives."

IN 1994, I WAS A PART-TIME SOLDIER, AND I WAS RACING FOR MY LITTLE EAST BERLIN CYCLING TEAM, THE BERLINER TSC. The Berlin Wall had been down for five years, but a lot of the infrastructures were still in place. Essentially the team was an extension of my old sports school, and it was sponsored by the military; hence the soldiering aspect. In the old West Berlin there was a good team, the Opel-Schüler Berlin, that we raced against in all the regional and national races. It was run by Hans Jaroszewicz, who twice rode the Tour de France for Germany, back when the race was still organized by national teams.

Then one day at a race, a teammate mentioned that Jaroszewicz had a good-looking daughter. I remember saying at first, "Hans? A good-looking daughter? Nah, that's not possible!" And then he pointed across the parking lot and said, "Well, look!"

And when I did, I just said, "Wow, *that* is his daughter?!" For the longest time, I never had an opportunity to chat with her, not even at the local races, where everybody knew each other. But one day, we were both at a race in northern Germany, the Internationale Niedersachsen-Rundfahrt. I was on the national team at the time, and she was there with her father's team. The race started way up north on this island called Norderney, and since my parents lived in the north of Germany, they drove me up to the start. And who did they happen to park next to? Hans Jaroszewicz's daughter, Stephanie.

I had a lot of gear and luggage to unload and take to my team car, but, suddenly, I realized that this was the moment. And I just said, "Hey! Hi, Stephanie! I'm Jens. Would you be kind enough to give me a hand and help me unload all this stuff?" She agreed, and soon enough, we started chatting.

Things started out slowly, though. The next day, it was just like, "Hi!" And the day after, "Hi! How are you?" But this was back in the amateur days, and it was really "roots" style. The entire race would often eat together in local gymnasiums or something, so we had time to talk and get to know each other that week. I was 23 and she was 24, and I was a lot younger in my head back then, just more childish. But I could tell by the way she smiled back at me that she didn't hate me!

Stephanie was training to become a massage therapist, so part of her role on the team was to give the riders massages after the race. Toward the end of the race, I was in the leader's jersey, and she even gave me a massage one night, which really gave us the chance to talk. It was my teammates, I think, who organized that for us, something I will be eternally grateful for! Then, on the last day, I ran into her after the stage, and she ripped off a corner of the brochure for the German League and wrote her phone number on it. It took me only a day to call her, but I kept that little piece of paper in my wallets for years, just as a souvenir.

I don't think her parents exactly approved of me. In the first years after the Berlin Wall came down, there was a fair amount of tension between West Germans and the old East Germans. Plus, I had my "Wayne Gretzky" mullet! But then a lot of parents don't think any guy is good enough for their daughters.

It was just a matter of time, however, before I wore them down. Eventually, they saw the man in the boy I was. It took Stephanie a little while to warm up to me, too. But I was insistent! Finally, I got a date with her and we went out to dinner. I remember thinking that, to be politically correct, it would be best to meet her in the middle of the city, so I proposed a restaurant at Alexanderplatz, in between the old east and west sides of town. I don't know if I kissed her that night, but we did have an ice cream for two, which was pretty romantic in my eyes!

Things did move along quickly after we first started dating, fast enough that our first son, Marc, was born just a year-and-a-half after we first met, when I was still an amateur. And he proved to be just the first in a long line of Voigts, one that didn't stop until 2011, when our sixth child, Helen, was born.

I remember Helen's birth well because I had to miss the team presentation of my newly founded Leopard Trek team. When my teammates left for the first early-season training camp, I was in the maternity ward of our hospital in Berlin.

The father inside me, of course, would not have been anywhere else. There was just no question of where I wanted to be. No matter if it's your first or your sixth child, every time is special, and it's never routine.

Our fifth child, Maya, had a very difficult birth. Essentially, her umbilical cord was wrapped around her neck three times. As a result, every time contractions occurred, she would strangle herself. It was terrible. The midwife sensed that there was trouble, but the doctors waited way too long before coming to the same conclusion.

Right when I went out to get some tea for my wife and some coffee for me, the doctor pushed the alarm button for an emergency c-section. As I stood there in the hall with the tea and coffee in my hand, they rushed by me with my wife into the operating room. About fifteen additional doctors and nurses showed up and everybody was in a rush, so nobody had time to explain anything to me because they were focused on saving my child's life. I remember it took only seven-and-a-half minutes from the pushing of the alarm button until Maya was born. And yes, even as a non-doctor, I could see that it was a last-second save. Fortunately, Maya was a strong little fighter and she survived, but that night, I thought I might lose both my wife and my baby.

Stephanie recovered a lot quicker than Maya, who had to stay in the hospital for a month. They used a new technology on her. The clinic put her on a cooling bed to slow down the metabolism in order to avoid any damaging swelling of her brain. I had to go home and tell my other four children that everything was going to be fine, that their mum would just be staying in the hospital for a few extra days. Those first days I was driving my wife around the hospital in her hospital bed and, later, in a wheelchair, until she recovered enough that she could walk again.

Back then my day started at 5 am, when I woke and drove straight to the hospital to see my wife and my daughter, reading books to her so she would know that we were there and that she was not alone. I would drive home around 6:30 to wake up the other kids and, together with my mother-in-law, get them ready for school. Afterward I would make some phone calls, answer some emails, or squeeze in an hour on the home trainer with the phone next to me. Then I'd pick up all the kids up from school again, help them with their homework, and in the late afternoon, drive back to the hospital to see my wife and my daughter again. Then it was back home to feed the kids their dinner and get them to bed. After they all fell asleep, I went one last time to the hospital to say goodnight to my wife and my daughter. And all the time I had to keep a smile on my face in front of my other four children so that they wouldn't be afraid.

After the first night, the doctors said "we hope but cannot guarantee that she will survive." After five days, they said "she will survive but we don't know yet if she can hear or see." After two weeks, the doctors said "we know she can hear because she reacts to noises, but we don't know if she is able to see." And after three weeks, they said "we know she will be able to see, but we are not sure yet if she will be able to walk or to speak or write or to attend a normal school." After Maya was released from hospital, we had to go back there on a daily basis, then every other day, then once a week, once a month. Believe it or not, it was only last year, when Maya started school and was 7 years old, that we finally got released from the special surveillance program and the doctors confirmed what we already knew: that Maya is a perfectly fine and beautiful young girl. My wife and I were really grateful to live in country with great doctors and a great healthcare system. That's one of the reasons I never moved to Switzerland or Monaco to save on taxes. Taxes in Germany are high because they pay for our hospitals, schools, museums, and police forces. Without taxpayers, we would not have such a great healthcare system, and who knows how it all might have ended up for little Maya. Today she is a beautiful, happy girl, a great lover of animals, and doing great in life. My wife and I know that life has been good to us. It's been far from easy, but it all turned out absolutely great. And ever since our experience with Maya, we always remember to put things in perspective. Life is all about having the right priorities, isn't it?!

After that experience, I knew I had to be there for Helen's birth. The births of my children are the only moments in life when I always cry. I'm a grown-up man. I don't cry for victories, nothing. But I do cry when each kid arrives. There's always a tear in my eye. It's just a special moment. And as much as I love being on the road at the races or at some special event, there's nothing like turning the key of your house after you've been on the road for a week or two and having your kids come running and jumping into your arms. It's in those moments that you feel most "alive."

That said, you never can plan on having six children. Sometimes, I do pinch myself and go, "Jensie, what were you thinking?" I remember back in my early days as a professional when I was rooming with Chris Boardman. We talked a lot about the differences of growing up in a capitalist or communist state, but we also talked a lot about our families. I'll never forget the time Chris first told me that he already had four children. I just blurted out, "Chris! Are you insane? What are you thinking? Your life is over! Why did you do that?"

And Chris just laughed, shook his head, and said, "Man, you're just a silly young kid. You don't know!"

Years later, I remember sending him a text saying, "Hey, Chris, I'm catching up. I've got four kids now!"

He responded, "If you could just see Sally [Boardman's wife] and me laughing right now after you gave me so much grief! Do you remember when you said my life was over?"

And I was like, "Yes, I do remember, Chris. Yes, I do."

But then the best came after Helen was born. I sent another message to Chris saying, "I've got six kids now. I finally caught up!"

He responded, "No, my son. You will always come in second to me. I'm on holiday with my six children and my pregnant wife!" At that point, I just gave up. I never could compete with Chris!

It's true that I always wanted a big family. I had an older brother and a younger sister. So yes, I wanted to have several kids. But six? Like I said, you can't plan for that! I remember saying to Stephanie after our third kid, "Hey, maybe we should stop? We have three kids just like my parents had. That was nice." And then we had four and I said, "Hey, Stephanie, maybe we should stop. Four is nice. We have two boys and two girls. It's a nice round number." But as you can see, we just continued!

So now, we have six little and not-so-little Voigts running around. All six are real Voigts. And as I sometimes say jokingly, they all come from the same production line. In all six, you can see a bit of Stephanie and a bit of me. They all have blue eyes like Stephanie. And like me, they were all very blond when they were young. The boys tend to have my chin and nose, but fortunately the girls don't, because my chin is pretty, how shall we say, manly. And my nose is, well, pretty much like an orange squeezer.

Marc, the oldest, is like Stephanie. He's very clean, neat, and organized, and he doesn't like endurance sports. He prefers team sports because he's very social, and he's always been a big lacrosse enthusiast.

Julian is more like me. He can't stand team sports. The idea of chasing a soccer ball around with 20 kids would drive him up a wall. He is tall and lanky, like me, and likes endurance sports, especially mountain biking. And like his dad, he thinks that tidiness and orderliness are only for small-minded people. The geniuses of the world control the chaos. For years, everything in his room was on the ground. He just said, "Hey, if it's on the ground, I can see where it is!"

Adriana is a bit of a mix. She can be strong-minded like her father, and she has a bit of my temper, too. I know the public doesn't see it much, but in many ways, cycling saved the world from a real monster. All those years, I was able to channel my hostility. All those years, I was getting paid to hurt other people. I was getting paid to erase my demons. Where do I go with my demons now? I mean, how long can I keep them in a cage? So Adriana is a bit like me. She's struggling with her demons. They're out on the streets all the time as she becomes a teenager.

Kimmy is the perfect mix of Stephanie and me. Her face is the perfect mix, too. She is really athletic. She rode her first bike without training wheels before her third birthday. She walked at a really young age and as a young kid, just wasn't afraid of anything. She picks up every sport very easily. But on the flip side, she doesn't have the patience for any of them. She has tried a lot of sports, even horseback riding and hip-hop dancing. She picks everything up very quickly but then loses interest. For the moment, she is most motivated by school. She does well in school and is really driven to succeed.

Maya is only just starting school, so it's too early to tell where life will take her. Heck, it was only a year ago that she got a clean bill of health. She has a ton of energy and likes sports.

And finally, there's little Helen! Oh my, she's so cute. And my, oh my, she has so much energy. She's so wild, and she has a strong head. She must be a bit like me, because she doesn't like to share food. She'll get really aggressive when people try her food, but she's always trying to get other people's food. And you know, after all those years on the road, eating at the team table, I can tell you that I don't like to share my food, either! And like her dad, she's always hungry. If you give her a choice between eating chocolate or steak, she'll always choose the steak!

Although it's still too early to tell where my children's lives will lead them, I think it's safe to say that none of them are future "Jensies" destined for the professional peloton. Each one of my kids is unique in his or her own way, but I don't see any Tour de France participants in the lot.

BAD FOOD, BAD HOTELS

"It was always the same thing:
haricots verts (green beans), overcooked pasta,
and a chewy piece of meat!"

FROM THE OUTSIDE, BEING A PRO CYCLIST LOOKS EXCITING, I'M SURE. And sometimes, yes, it is. But often, from the inside, the life can be much less glamorous than expected. Actually, one of the best-kept secrets in the peloton is that the key to a long, successful career isn't hard training, but an athlete's ability to endure an endless line of bad hotels and bad food when on the road.

Finding a hotel big enough for all the riders and staff, with a parking lot for all the team buses and trucks, isn't always easy when you're out racing. But sometimes, we get some real dives! And I'm not just talking about my early years as a young pro. Heck, I got one of the worst rooms ever in my very last year as a professional in 2014. We were in Spain at the Ruta del Sol (Ciclista a Andalucia), and I woke with this strange feeling. I thought, "Oh man, why is my head itching so much? Why is my body itching?" My roommate, Bob Jungels, must have heard me moving around and said, "What's going on?" We turned on the light and found that our room had been attacked by ants! It was the middle of the night, and we were in the middle of the race. We couldn't believe it. There were ants everywhere. I had at least 10 in my hair, 20 on my body, and another 20 all over my bed!

There were no more rooms available in the hotel that night, so we just did the best we could. We tried to move our beds out of the way of what seemed to be the ants' little own auto route, but it was anything but a good night's sleep. To make matters worse, the team was booked in the same hotel the following night. We complained, and they assured us they would fix the problem, but we were in the same room the next night. The ants were gone, so I imagine that they must have fumigated very heavily. And I just had to ignore whatever kind of chemical residue we were breathing in as we slept that night.

You would have thought that in my nearly 20 years as a professional, hotels would have improved. And in some ways, they did. But as you can see, not always! Putting up with the bad hotels was easier in the early years, because we basically didn't know any better. Back in the day, bike racing was still pretty much confined to four or five countries, primarily France, Italy, Belgium, Holland, and Spain. And after growing up in East Germany, I was used to Spartan accommodations. So I wasn't shocked. It wasn't until we started doing races like the Tour of California that we saw something different. Suddenly, we were like, "Wow! They have hotels like that?! They have beds like that?!" UNBELIEVABLE!

I guess of all the countries we raced in regularly, Spain probably had the worst reputation when it came to hotels, and, in particular, on the island of Majorca. Now Majorca is a beautiful island in the Mediterranean, and as a result, there is a huge tourist turnover on a weekly basis.

And for some reason, Majorca is just known for fleas. We spent a lot of time in Majorca over the years, as a lot of teams do training camps there and there are good early-season races. There are a lot of good reasons to go to Majorca as a cyclist, but not for the fleas!

Racing in Spain did have one distinct advantage—the late race starts. Everything in that country is shifted back a couple of hours, so races generally start later, which is a real treat! I really liked being able to sleep in. Ever since I've been a father, sleeping in at home has not really been an option. So I look forward to racing in Spain, because it offers me one of those rare occasions to sleep in.

Each country had its individual characteristics. In Belgium, you know that you're going to be stuck racing in the wind and rain a lot. But you also know that, every once in a while, you can treat yourself to one of those amazing beers, of which they have hundreds. And then, of course, there are the fans, who are some of the best in the world! On any given day of the week, the fans come out in big numbers for the bike race. And they're all knowledgeable. They're all experts! At the end of my career, I would have fans in Belgium come up to me with the most amazing scrapbooks. They would have these books with every one of my team postcards signed by me. There were all kinds of articles about me that they had cut out over the years. They really put their hearts into it.

Holland was even worse when it came to the wind, probably because we often raced on these bike paths that were about 50 centimeters wide! The racing there is always so nervous, so sketchy and dangerous. But the Dutch probably had the best hotels in Europe, not to mention a lot of great American TV shows. So I would go to Holland to work on my English!

In Italy, you knew the hotel rooms would be small. But you also knew that the food would be good and that the coffee would be even better. I don't know how they do it, but in Italy, even the gas stations have awesome coffee.

France was just the opposite. They had the worst pasta. And the coffee was pretty bad, too. I swear, in France, if your team dinner was scheduled for eight o'clock, they would put the pasta in to boil at noon! I'm not kidding here. I would swear to this and agree to have lightning hit me if I'm exaggerating in the slightest. The French just seem to have this amazing disregard for pasta! And as a bike racer, you get pretty sensitive about your pasta! You know, it's almost funny. The French are so famous for their cooking. But in the hotels we stayed in, it was always the same thing: haricots verts (green beans), overcooked pasta, and a chewy piece of meat!

How could this be, you ask? Well, like most things in life, it comes down to money. It's up to the race organizers to pay for the hotels and the food, so such things are dependent on the race organizer's budget. If a race organizer says to a hotel owner, I can only pay you four euros per rider per dinner, then the hotel has to come up with a menu that fits the budget. The hotel wants to make some money, too. So if, say, the organizer pays four euros for dinner, the hotel may well take one euro profit, which in reality leaves only three euros for a meal. As a result, you're going to get the cheapest meat, the cheapest haricots verts, and a lot of overcooked pasta!

In most hotels, we wouldn't eat in the main restaurant but rather in a conference room of some kind. A lot of fans probably thought that this was to maintain privacy, but in the eyes of the riders, there was another reason altogether. Neither the race organizer nor the hotel wanted the riders to see what was really being served!

This, of course, was all before the teams got their own cooking trucks with private chefs and everything. Inevitably, the teams or the riders themselves would break down and buy regular food from the restaurant because, well, a bike racer cannot live on haricots verts and overcooked pasta alone!

On more than one occasion—and I'm not just talking about France here—I've seen someone from the team, sometimes even myself, go up to the restaurant owner and say, "Look at this! Would you really feed this to your own children?" Of course, the owner would say no, which only begged the questions, "Why do you think you can give this food to us, then? Are we just animals to you?"

France did have its upsides, too, especially when we were able to get some cheese. It may be a bit of a cliché, but the baguettes and cheeses in France are just amazing. Still, to this day, I love to dip a crispy baguette into a cup of coffee in the morning. Modern sports science really frowns on eating white bread, but that baguette and coffee combo is just one of those things I've come to love from my life on the road. And a baguette, cheese, and fresh grapes are a pretty good way to end just about any meal.

The other thing you have to get used to on the road is spending countless hours in your hotel room. It would be really scary to count up all the hours we cyclists spend sitting in our hotel rooms. But in all fairness, I guess you could say that it's something we spend our whole lives preparing for. It comes with the job, and you grow into it.

As an amateur, as a kid, you drive home from races every night. And then as you move up in the ranks, you start having shorter stage races where you might have two or three nights in a hotel. And then, when you go to training camps, you get in the habit of just hanging out. So you slowly get into it.

One thing I noticed that changed over the years was that riders really started staying in their rooms. Before, when I was starting out, whole teams—especially the Italian and Spanish teams—would hang out in the hotel lobby or by the pool or simply the parking lot after dinner or whenever there was some downtime. But cycling is like society, and now it seems that everybody spends the whole time roaming the Internet on their smartphones or tablets.

And now with social media, news travels so much faster. As a result, it seems that everybody knows where our hotel is. So today, a lot more journalists and fans hang around the hotel, and as soon as you look like you've got nothing to do, it's as though you're extending an open invitation for an interview or autographs or whatever. Often, it seems your room is the only place where you can really just chill and be left alone.

That said, I never minded hanging out in my room. Obviously, I always have a lot of action at home with all the kids, so I welcomed the chance to simply relax. Also, I'm really good at falling asleep in the afternoon. I'm actually world-class when it comes to taking naps. Plus, I always liked to read a lot or play a computer game or something. Or, back in the day, I would watch Bobby Julich do his stretching or core-muscle training on the fit ball. And, of course, I would make fun of him. I just couldn't get my head around it. Stretching made sense, but I guess I just put it in the "too hard" basket or category. Bobby and I also had a lot of deep conversations about how we saw life, family, and other matters. And if I wanted a little excitement, I could always go over to one of the Australians' rooms. Those guys always had a full stereo-entertainment system hooked up and going. So, for me, the hotel has always offered a rare opportunity for some downtime.

Now your ability to relax also depends on the hotel you're booked in. And that can be pretty hit or miss. Never is this more true than in the Tour de France. The Tour, you see, has its own points system for the hotels, and they try to work it out so each team in the race has the same hotel points by the end of the race. A really nice hotel is three points, while the not-so-nice hotels are one point. So you really have to make the most of the good hotels, because if you're in a beautiful château on a lake one night, you know that you'll likely be in some dive on a highway for the next two nights.

Travel, too, is a huge part of our existence as cyclists. That's one aspect of cycling that has definitely improved over the years, mostly due to the introduction of team buses. Back when I was starting out, we could spend hours cramped up in a team car after a stage—not the best way to recover from a hard race. But with the team buses, we can relax, spread out, and exchange war stories from the day's race. It's actually quite enjoyable!

Undoubtedly, the best day on the team bus is the last day of the Tour de France. The last stage of the Tour is always short, but the day is really long. We ride slowly for much of the race, and then there's all the postrace ceremony and the promenade down the Champs-Élysées. I'll never forget the first time I finished the Tour. I almost bonked on the final stage because it just took so long. But now we're prepared for that, and we always have a big pizza party waiting for us in the bus when we get back from the finish. What better way to end the Tour de France than with pizza and beer on the Place de la Concorde?

Who would have ever guessed that little old Jensie would someday have his own clothing brand! (James Startt)

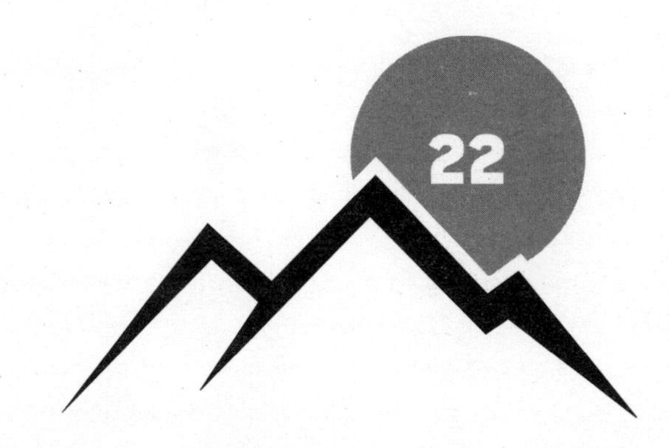

THE CULT OF JENS

"Jens for President!"

Jens as seen by Bobby Julich (longtime roommate and friend on Crédit Agricole and CSC; currently works for Team BMC):

You know, a lot of guys have the ability to turn on the charm when somebody important is around. But Jens has so much energy to talk to everyone, to share details of his life and genuinely ask about theirs. I don't know how he does it.

I'll never forget after the Tour of Georgia in 2004, Jens came to my house up in the mountains outside Reno for an altitude training camp to get ready for the Tour de France. Near the end, he asked to take my car into town to get some gifts for his kids.

But when he came back, he was just wasted. Now, normally, Jens is "Mr. Energy," but on this day, he just looked gone. He had this dark cloud around him.

I was like, "What happened? Did you wreck the car?"

"No," he said. "But I got nothing done!"

"What do you mean?" I said.

And he responded, "I got nothing done because everywhere I went people said, 'Hello! How are you?'"

And I said, "Yeah, and?"

To which he responded, "Yeah, so I had to talk to everybody in every store I went into for 15 or 20 minutes."

I had to laugh. "Jens," I said, "When an American says, 'Hi, how are you?' when you walk into a store, it's just a formality. It's like they're waving to you. They're not looking for your life story!"

But he was so distraught. "But I can't just do that. I can't just say 'fine.' I have to ask how they are doing, too, and then one thing leads to another, and we're having a conversation!"

But that's Jens. He genuinely likes people. He is a genuinely nice guy. Going out with him and trying to actually get something done is never easy, because he'll always end up talking to somebody. It doesn't matter if it's the CEO of a big company, a sponsor, or just somebody walking down the street. He gives everyone time. He always finds time to say hello. And it's not just a wave. He'll tell you a story or something, get you laughing, and then move on. But he makes people feel good. And he always leaves a mark.

IN THE LAST COUPLE OF YEARS OF MY CAREER, I WAS DEFINITELY LOSING STRENGTH. It was getting harder to win, and it was even getting hard to make the breakaways. But one thing that was undeniable was that my popularity just kept rising.

I was already pretty popular in France after racing on so many Tours de France and racing on a French team early in my career. I remember one headline in France called me "Father Courage," a word play on the Bertolt Brecht play *Mother Courage and Her Children*, for all my attacking. And, in Spain, they sometimes called me the "Boeing 747" for my ability to launch a breakaway.

Fans in the United States started picking up on me a bit later, but I remember in the 2009 Tour of California, while in the middle of a time trial, I looked up and saw someone wearing a "Jens for President" T-shirt. Bjarne was driving support behind me that day, and he pulled up and motioned to me in a way that said, "Did you see that guy's T-shirt?" Hilarious, just hilarious!

One day during the 2011 Tour of Colorado, I was in a big break, like a 12-man break, when out of nowhere, an official race car pulled up alongside of us, and suddenly baseball superstar Barry Bonds stuck his head out the window and yelled, "Go, Jens!" I was like, "WTF?!" There were 11 Americans in the group, and Barry Bonds was yelling for Jensie!

I first really understood the scope of the Jensie phenomenon in the 2011 Tour de France when, on a rest day, Stuart O'Grady, Fabian Cancellara, and the Schleck brothers set up a Twitter account for me along with Leopard Trek manager Brian Nygaard. First off, all the handles that I wanted were already taken. @shutuplegs was taken. @shutuplegs1 was taken. @shutuplegs2 was taken. Finally, we came up with @thejensie, and I amassed 10,000 followers in the first hour. It just kept going and growing! After two hours, I had nearly 40,000 followers.

This popularity is a result of a combination of things, not to mention some good luck. Part of it is that my way of talking, my humor, and my way of doing things just hit at the right moment. My funny way of speaking in English, it seems, was perfect for Twitter sound bites. And people really seem to appreciate the way I talk in metaphors all the time, and I'm always making analogies to cycling from real life. I've only been on Twitter for four years, but it was an instant success. My little one-liners don't translate the same way in a newspaper article, but they were perfect for Twitter. And the ability that social media has to disseminate information is just incredible. I've always enjoyed the fans and always treated them the same way, but suddenly, because of social media, I could say something sort of funny to one fan and thousands of people would know about it. That really changed the game. Back in 1998, if I talked to one person in France or Belgium and said, "If you only follow other people's footprints, then you never make your own footprints in the path of life," they might tell 10 or 15 people what I said. But with the rise of Twitter and Facebook, the whole world could hear about every little saying I came up with.

And it's true that I do have a plateful of one-liners. A few of my favorite are "Whatever makes the race wet and sticky is good for me!";

"If I'm hurting, then the others must be hurting twice as much as I am"; and "Start out simple, because life will get complicated enough by itself." Let's also not forget the one I co-opted from Chris Boardman—you know, the one that goes, "If you try to win, you might lose. But if you don't try to win, you'll lose for sure."

I hope that I can say I worked for this popularity. Certainly, part of my popularity was due to my success on the bike, and I worked very hard for that. I always walked the walk and stuck to my word. I'm reliable. I don't have a diamond earring. I don't have a fancy haircut. I don't have a fancy tattoo. And I don't live in Monaco—although sometimes I wish I did! No, I'm just a normal guy living in the country I grew up in. I have six children, all with the same wife. There is no patchwork. And with my mother-in-law living with us, three generations all live under the same roof here in Berlin. I even cut my own grass. So I'm just really normal and really reliable. I say what I do, and I do what I say. And I think with all the troubles in our sport, with superstars who come and go, people started to realize that Jensie was sort of the rock in the sea, the one thing you can count on in the sport. Tides come and go. Storms come and go. Waves come and go. But you know where the rock is. And you can put your foot on the rock.

And then the fact that I lasted so long probably didn't hurt my reputation any, either. A lot of people get into cycling late. And a lot of people in my age group are out cycling, and they can all look at me and go, "Look at Jensie. He's 41, 42, or 43, and he's still competitive." Heck, I still managed to win a stage in the Tour of Colorado at the age of 42. People my age know how hard it is to get into top shape as you get older, so I think a lot of people really came to respect the fact that I could still dish out some pain in the Tour de France even after I was 40.

RADIO SHACK

"I needed to squeeze everything out of my body so that I would have no regrets."

AFTER ANDY AND FRANK SCHLECK FINISHED SECOND AND THIRD IN THE TOUR DE FRANCE IN 2011, I WAS FEELING PRETTY GOOD ABOUT THE FUTURE OF MY LEOPARD TREK TEAM. No, we hadn't had a big win that first year together, but we were still very successful, and I was looking forward to building on that success in 2012. I would soon learn, however, that the narrative was about to change again.

As I had been doing since 2010, I followed up the Tour with two great races in the States, the Tour of Utah and the Tour of Colorado, both of which I'd really come to enjoy, as I always came out of the Tour de France in good condition, and I could race well there. And it was there that I learned that Leopard Trek would be no more and that the team was merging with Radio Shack.

I'll be honest—my first reaction to the news was far from positive. As you have seen in my life, I'm not a person who invites change for the sake of change. At that point, I had essentially changed teams only three times in my career. Leopard was my third team, and we had spent a lot of time and energy getting the team off the ground. So why change again? Why stop after barely six months? Give us a chance! Nobody cuts a tree down after two years. You have to give it a chance to grow. We had just planted the tree.

In addition, I didn't feel comfortable joining up with Radio Shack, a team that was run by Lance Armstrong's longtime director, Belgian Johan Bruyneel, who was increasingly coming under fire as the US Anti-Doping Agency investigation of Lance Armstrong evolved. This was late 2011. Armstrong's ex-teammate Floyd Landis had already launched his lawsuit against Armstrong, and news was constantly breaking regarding doping on the old US Postal team run by Bruyneel. And as I already mentioned, I twice refused to join Johan and Lance's teams because I was afraid that, if the rumors were true, I might be faced with pressure to dope, which I'd always avoided. I just didn't see a need to be associated with such things.

One morning, after breakfast at the Tour of Utah, I was sitting at the table with the Schleck brothers, and Frank asked me, "So, Jens, what do you really think about the merger?"

I said, "Are you kidding? You just opened the front door and let the devil back in! We're gonna run this whole beautiful project right into the wall! What are you thinking?" I didn't understand the need to associate ourselves with Bruyneel, who, as I said, was at the center of one of the biggest doping scandals to ever hit the sport, and one that was unraveling before our eyes. Nobody, at that very moment, was perceived more negatively in cycling than Johan Bruyneel, including Lance Armstrong.

It was not an easy time for us, and for a couple of weeks there was real tension between me and my longtime friends, the Schlecks. I really loved that year with Leopard, and to this day, one of the things I most regret in my career is the fact that the project didn't live longer, because we really did do a lot of things right. Heck, when I first signed with them, I was sure it was the team I would retire with.

Suddenly, late in the 2011 season, I found myself calling other teams just to see what my options were. Through my friend Bobby Julich, I made contact with Team Sky, as well as the new Australian team Orica-GreenEdge. But it was September already. Budgets were closing up quickly. I was at the end of my contract, and I was a 40-year-old cyclist. I still felt as though I had a place as a professional, and I still wasn't ready to retire. That said, finding a new place of employment was far from easy.

But Frank and Andy were privy to more information regarding the inner workings of the team than I was. After all, Leopard Trek was based in Luxembourg. It was built around them. Flavio Becca, a Luxembourg businessman, provided the financial support in the beginning, but he wasn't capable of underwriting the team forever. On the other side, Johan had two sponsors that he could bring to the table, Radio Shack and Nissan. And both teams were riding Trek bicycles, so from an economic and business point of view, the merger did make sense.

And on a personal level, I was offered a good contract, so soon enough, my decision to remain was pretty much resolved. After all, how many 40-year-old cyclists are offered a new contract when two teams are merging and roughly 40 riders are vying for no more than 30 spots? No doubt about it, I was very happy to have a job. Perhaps I was being selfish, but when that contract came in the mail, I was just plain relieved!

In the long term, things turned out great. The seeds of my last team, Trek Factory Racing, were planted here. And thanks to them, I couldn't have had a better end of my career. But in the short term, things were quite complicated.

First off, everyone clearly underestimated the challenge of bringing two teams together. Both teams had some big riders, not to mention a lot of staff. Bringing Leopard Trek together with Radio Shack–Nissan would be like merging, say, the NBA's Dallas Mavericks with the Los Angeles Lakers. That would definitely take more than a week! A lot of egos, strategies, and approaches have to come together before things start to jell. And in our case, things never really jelled that first year. In those first few months of the new team, nobody really knew who was in charge. Nobody understood the chain of command. There was a lot of mistrust between the two teams.

So much of a team's success comes down to operations and how people work together. Much of this goes unseen by spectators, but the daily workings of a team are quite complicated. For one, there is never one team, but rather two or three different squads racing different races at the same time. When one team is racing the Ardennes classics, like the Amstel Gold Race and Liège-Bastogne-Liège, another is at the Tour of Trentino in Italy and another may well be on their way to the Tour of Turkey. It's a highly complicated affair, and the entire staff must be in lockstep synchronization. Such things set the tone for the team, and often enough, results reflect just how well a team clicks.

Before the season even started, we were moving our team headquarters once more, and we spent much of the early season butting heads. Johan ran his team more like a business, whereas Leopard was more of a family affair. Both ways work, but not necessarily together. Some of the mechanics, for example, saw their job as more nine to five and really wanted to go home at a certain time, while others preferred to stay until the job was done. Mechanics, though, must work as a team, and it's not easy to work together with two very different approaches. As a result, we struggled to foster any kind of team spirit.

Perhaps on Leopard, we were a bit spoiled. If we asked for brown rice, we got brown rice. If we asked for white rice, we got white rice. If we asked for a mix of white rice and whole-grain rice, we got that, too. But suddenly, with Johan's team, it was more like rice is rice. Win some races and we can discuss different kinds of rice. But until then, you get rice!

It really wasn't until around June that we started to get things together and reached some kind of consensus, found some kind of balance.

And though I had my reservations about Johan, I have to say he ran a good ship. He worked well with the different staff members and was constantly looking for ways to bring the best out of the riders. Let's not forget, our goal was still to win the Tour de France. Frank and Andy Schleck were great riders, but neither had yet won the Tour de France at that time. Johan, for example, made the two brothers race separate programs so that they would race more independently. In the end, it didn't really work, but that's just an example of how he was trying to change things up, to break people out of their routines, with the hope that they would perform better. Later in the season, I remember he asked me to sit down with him and discuss how the team could be better. We were at a training camp in Belgium preparing for the world championship team time trial. He understood that things had not worked out well, and he wanted my input as an experienced rider. He got out a pencil and paper and started jotting things down, things that worked, things that didn't work. Until the day he was fired, he was still focused on making the team better. It was a good, constructive talk. But only weeks later the team announced that they were separating themselves from Johan, as his involvement in doping with the US Postal team became increasingly clearer.

Despite all the chaos on the Radio Shack–Nissan team in 2012, I had a very good year. Physically, I was still on top of my game. I won a stage in the Tour of Catalonia, and I got fifth in Paris-Nice. Then, in the Tour de France, my teammate Fabian Cancellara won the prologue in Liège, Belgium, and wore the yellow jersey for the first week. Situations like that are perfect for me because, well, they give me something to do. Whenever you have a teammate in the race lead, it's up to your team to control the race. On any given stage, there will be an early breakaway that tries their chances. Many times, I'm in breakaways like that, but when my team has the yellow jersey, my role is very different, and I have to ride a steady tempo on the front as much as possible to make sure that the breakaways don't gain too much time. It's one of the things I love doing the most in the sport. I take real pride in defending a leader's jersey, and if I say so myself, I think I do a good job at it. Heck, I probably spent at least 250 kilometers on the front that first week of the Tour, pulling the peloton through the countryside. But even after Fabian lost the yellow jersey, my job was not done. In the final week of the Tour, my team was winning the overall team standings, a very coveted prize. The team prize is awarded to the team with the five highest-placed riders in the race. And I was the fifth-best-placed rider on the team. As a result, I was constantly chasing down breaks and trying to get in breakaways myself to keep my overall place as high as possible.

I was really happy with my Tour that year and came out of it strongly, which set me up for the end of the season. Just a couple of weeks after the 2012 Tour, I went to the United States and won a stage in the Tour of Colorado. So ironically, even though there were a lot of bumps in the road, personally, I had a very good year, and well before the end of the season, I had a contract for another year, which I must say was very satisfying.

Sometimes, people wonder how I managed to keep my motivation so high year in and year out. Well, first off, there's the small matter of having six children to provide for at home. That provides plenty of motivation. But there are other reasons, as well.

You know, even after I was a well-established professional, I never took my place in the peloton for granted. And although I'm sure many of my fellow professionals won't like hearing this, I think that one-year contracts are a good source of motivation. With a one-year contract, your ass is constantly on the line. Most contracts are completed around the time of the Tour de France or in August at the latest. So if you haven't had some good results by that point, you know that you're in trouble. Later in my career, many of my contracts were one-year deals, so I constantly needed to prove myself. By that point, it is safe to say that I knew my body very well. I knew what I needed to do during the winter to set myself up for a good start to the season, and I always made sure that I did it.

I think it's safe to say that most people think of me as a pretty happy-go-lucky guy, and on the outside, I often am. But I'm also my own worst critic. I'm very critical of myself, and I've even been known to hold grudges against myself. And on a very personal level, the last thing I wanted was to call myself a quitter for the rest of my life simply because I stopped racing too early. I know that may sound funny or strange coming from an over-40-year-old rider, but that's just the way I'm wired! Over the years, I saw a lot of cyclists who, for one reason or another, retired too early. Often a rider would get caught without a team at the end of the season, but sometimes riders were simply burned out and wanted a change. Regardless of the reason, most riders who retire too early regret it for a long time afterward. And knowing myself, I don't know that I would ever have really gotten over such frustration. It would have come back to haunt me for years to come!

I always have been a big fan of the idea that one is the master of his own destiny, that you hold your life and your faith in your hands. And when it came to my own retirement, I wanted to control the situation. I wanted it to be my decision. But to do that, I needed to squeeze everything out of my body so that I would have no regrets when I walked away. One of the satisfactions of my career was that I ended it on my own terms. And I can tell you that I will never, ever feel the desire to make a comeback. I went as far and as long as I could. And now I simply don't want to hurt or suffer anymore.

Perhaps the fact that I turned professional late, that I struggled to find my first professional contract, also played into this mind-set. I was always well grounded enough to realize the amazing opportunity I had simply to be a professional. I mean, in the years you spend as a professional, you're a rock star. You're traveling all over the world. People are helping you out with everything. Okay, I might not be Mick Jagger. But hey, it's a great life! I would be lying if I said that I didn't enjoy it, so I wasn't going to take it for granted.

And this may sound like vanity, but one tremendous source of satisfaction late in my career was simply knowing I was still good enough to make the cut, still good enough to make the Tour de France team, and still good enough to get a contract. Making the cut was ingrained in me from a very young age, from my days in the East German sports school. It's second nature to me. And looking back over my career, I have to say that I'm very proud of the fact that I was good enough to compete in the Champions League of my sport for 17 years.

Another element of motivation was the Tour de France. From my first years as a professional, I fell in love with the Tour. Starting out on French teams, it was just impossible not to be bitten by the bug. Heck, many French teams more or less exist *just* for the Tour. But strictly from a business standpoint, the Tour is key, because that's the race with the highest international visibility. And since it lasts for three weeks, your presence and performance, and hence your market value, are only magnified by it. That's three weeks of visibility on prime-time television all around the world. How many races can offer that? So doing the Tour always remained a huge objective. While winning became more difficult with age, there were still a lot of roles for me in the Tour de France as a team rider, be it riding tempo for Fabian if he got the yellow jersey early in the race or pacing the Schlecks up some of the climbs. I was a pillar and a playmaker. As I have said, one of my great strengths has always been my reliability. It didn't matter what the weather was like or what was going on in the race, my team directors always knew that I would be where I needed to be at any moment in the race. And in the Tour de France, such reliability is a real commodity.

Alone again, this time on Stage 5 of the Critérium du Dauphiné in 2014. It was in moments like this where I really started feeling my age as it got harder and harder to bridge the gaps. (James Startt)

THE ART OF THE LONG BREAKAWAY

"I'm not slowing down for any raindrops here!"

Jens as seen by Lars Michaelsen (onetime teammate and sports director to Voigt, currently sports director on the Tinkoff–Saxo Bank team):

Going to a bike race with Jens is like going to a bike race with a poker player. Jens is always looking at his hand and seeing what he can do with it, for himself and for his team. Sometimes he might launch an attack and go for the win. Sometimes he might attack just for a couple of strategic bonus seconds. Sometimes he might attack to go after the best-climber jersey or some other smaller prize. Or, perhaps, he would start driving the pace after more than 180 kilometers of racing, simply to split up the field and set up one of his teammates. Regardless of the prize, he's always trying to make the most of what he's got, for himself as well as the team, always trying to make the most out of every situation with the cards he is holding at the time.

But the one thing you can count on is that, whenever he goes, whatever the prize, however big or small, Jens is going to make a full-on, 100-percent-committed effort. He's not always the easiest rider to direct because, well, he's constantly forcing you to improvise with him. Sometimes, I'll be honest, I'm not sure where he's going with a move. Sometimes he makes a move that appears to be nothing less than suicidal. But Jens is always thinking on the bike. He has real tactical sense that often gets overlooked. And sometimes he can almost will something to happen with pure and utter commitment.

I was in the car directing the day he won that amazing stage in the Tour of Colorado in 2012, and I'll be the first to admit I really did not see an early solo move working. He did, though, and he proved it. But there were many other, smaller moves that demonstrate how he was always thinking, always calculating.

Take the first stage in his final Tour de France in 2014. He gets in a three-man breakaway on the first stage, a flat stage, knowing full well that there is very little chance that the breakaway will stay away with all the sprint teams eager to have a field sprint. So then he looks at his hand to see what his other options are, and he focuses on the best-climber jersey. After losing the sprint on top of the first climb, though, he understands that he is not the best climber. So he has to come up with another tactic. Suddenly, he launches a big attack, drops the others, and picks up the bonus points on the next two climbs to get the polka-dot jersey. He knew that he would only keep the jersey for a day, most likely, but it didn't matter. He was just making the most out of the cards that he was holding at the time.

I THINK IT'S SAFE TO SAY THAT A LARGE PART OF MY REPUTATION WAS BUILT AROUND MY SEEMINGLY INSATIABLE APPETITE FOR GOING INTO LONG BREAKAWAYS. Just by the law of averages, the chance of a breakaway staying away until the finish is always slim, and more times than not, going in an early break is nothing short of a suicide move. Because of the low odds, a lot of cyclists never even try for the early moves. But if everyone thought like that, the sport would just be so boring. And on a personal level, I would have won a lot fewer races.

So I learned early on that the breakaway offered me a unique opportunity to exploit some of my strengths and would often represent my best opportunities for personal success. In addition, you generally put your teammates in a good position when you're in a breakaway, because as long as someone on your team is up the road in a breakaway, everyone else on the team can pretty much sit back. They can say, "Hey, we've got somebody in the front group, so we don't have to work or chase here!" It's a win-win situation, really, and it brought me some of my most memorable wins.

Without a doubt, one of my greatest moments came in the 2006 Tour de France when I won the stage to Montélimar. It was my last victory in the Tour de France and remains a highlight to this day. Stage 13 was the longest stage of the Tour that year, stretching 230 kilometers from Béziers to Montélimar. As the winner, I covered the distance in 5:24:36 at an average speed of 42.573 kilometers an hour. But those are just the pure facts, and the race was actually a lot more interesting than that because, well, it changed the shape of the entire race. We actually finished the day with a 30-minute gap on the peloton, one of the largest winning margins in recent history, and it allowed Spaniard Oscar Pereiro to take over the yellow jersey.

But what a hard stage it was! Actually, the whole Tour had been hard. Just waking up was hard. I remember my roommate Bobby Julich just saying one morning, "Oh man, every morning, you lie in bed more dead than alive because every day you went over your limits. Sometimes you just look like a beached whale, lying on your bed totally passed out!"

And the morning of that stage was no exception. I was the last to wake up, the last to go down for breakfast, the last to finish packing, and needless to say, the last to get on the team bus. Once in the bus, we had the team meeting. The director asked, "Who wants to go for the breakaway today?" And, suddenly, all eyes were on me.

Needless to say, I was riding right next to the red car of Tour de France director Christian Prudhomme as we cruised through the neutral zone toward the official start. And needless to say, I was one of the first riders to attack.

But everyone knew that this was a perfect day for a breakaway, and for many, it would be a last chance, as we were soon entering the Alps for the final week of hard racing. As a result, there were a lot of attacks, and it took a long time for the breakaway to get away. Actually, I almost missed the move!

At one point, I saw four riders getting away. I could sense that the peloton was giving up and slowing down and realized this was a make-or-break moment. I had to act immediately to have even a little chance to catch the four riders. We must have had a little tailwind, because I remember I was in my biggest gear, a 53 x 11, until I caught them about two or three kilometers later. I was still at the peak of my career, so failing or not catching them never really crossed my mind. But once I reached the back wheel of the last rider, I was hurting all over my body. I was hurting so bad, *I COULD FEEL THE LACTIC ACID IN MY EARLOBES!* I swear, I could not speak right. All I could do was make some gestures to say that I could not possibly pull through, not for a few minutes at least.

And when I had a chance to check out who exactly my breakaway companions were, I just thought to myself, "Okay, for sure the pack won't catch us, but this is going to be a difficult stage to win here."

Four really strong riders were in the group: Oscar Pereiro from Spain, Manuel Quinziato from Italy, Andriy Grivko from Ukraine, and Sylvain Chavanel from France, whom I feared the most. We worked well together, and soon enough, we understood that we were gone for good, and that one of us would be the winner of the day.

In many ways, our breakaway was the classic breakaway. It consisted of three parts: the full-gas start to get away, a long midsection where you just ride along the countryside working together, and the final part where our little brotherhood falls apart as individuals start attacking.

The midsection can sometimes be boring. But there are also funny moments. I remember on this day, as the gap was increasing, I kept telling Pereiro that we were going to ride him into the yellow jersey. He was the best-placed rider in the group. And as the gap increased from 10 minutes to 20 minutes to 30 minutes, so did his chances. Oscar didn't say much. He just responded with a grin.

Grivko was the first to attack, but he was quickly swallowed up and dropped. As predicted, Sylvain Chavanel was really attacking us hard, but then finally, with about five kilometers to go, I managed to get clear with Pereiro on my wheel. I pulled as long as possible, until I felt it was safe to swoop off and let Oscar pull as well.

Going into the sprint, I tried to remember some very basic golden rules when it comes to sprinting. The first is, close off one side. Why? Because that way you only have to turn your head in one direction to watch your opponent, as the barriers on one side serve to block any surprise moves from that side. So I rode as close to barriers as I dared, nearly touching the clapping hands of the spectators. That only left the windy side open for Oscar to attack. Since I had more trust in my raw power rather than pure speed at the end of a long stage, I slowed down and delayed the sprint until almost 75 meters from the line. And then I just went full force, accelerating toward the finish.

Now, often, people think the first position is the weaker position in a two-up sprint, but the rider in the first position dictates the rhythm. He decides what happens, so I often prefer to lead out the sprint. Plus, as stupid as it might sound, I always thought that, since the rider on my wheel is already behind me, he is already a bike length behind. The way I look at it, I just have to stay in front.

My plan worked out, and Oscar could not get up the speed to pass me before we crossed the line. Still, though, I didn't raise my arms until after the line. That is one thing I just never do, and I would simply kill myself for losing a race by celebrating too early.

It was a long, very hot day in the saddle, and the peloton was also paralyzed by the heat and the yellow jersey. Floyd Landis, who was wearing the yellow jersey at that time, refused to make his team work until it was too late. In the end, we gained 29:57 minutes over the peloton, enough to give Oscar the yellow jersey. Everybody expected Oscar to lose it soon after, but he went on to win that Tour. And I was there when we wrote tour history.

People sometimes ask me about that day, if we made some sort of deal. But by looking at the TV images, you can see we were just going full gas to the line. Early in the stage, I jokingly said, "Okay, if we arrive together, I'll take the stage, and Oscar, you take the yellow jersey." But once we went clear in the last couple of kilometers, we still didn't know if we really had enough time to put Oscar in yellow. After all, he was nearly 30 minutes behind the yellow jersey at the start of the stage. As a result, both of us really wanted the stage win. There was no deal or serious talk between us. Anyway, I was never a big fan of deals. I never sold a race, and I never bought a race. I did give away some races for good reasons—like the one stage in the Tour of Italy that I already mentioned—but never for money. That was somehow never attractive to me.

But I must say, that day worked out perfectly for both of us, and until this day, every time I see Oscar, we just look at each other and smile. We became friends after suffering together for more than five-and-a-half hours in the heat in France that day. And it was a great day for both of us.

In 2010, I had one of those rare moments when, in the middle of the race, I could look into a crystal ball and see the future. It came in the 2010 Tour of Catalonia. Stage 4 finished on this circuit that we covered a couple of times before the finish. A breakaway had gotten away earlier in the day and was still dangling off the front as we came onto this climb, the Alt de la Josa del Cadí. It was on this wide road into a big headwind, and you could see the breakaway about a minute up the road. I was riding next to Christian Vande Velde and Levi Leipheimer, and I said, "Hey, guys, in a perfect world, I will attack at exactly this spot next lap, bridge up to the break, then ride with them for a bit to recover before dropping them all at the finish." They both just sort of looked at me and laughed.

But that's pretty much what I did. A lap later, I just went full gas. As in my vision, I caught up with the front group and worked with them for a while before dropping them. Over the summit, I really attacked the downhill along with Rein Taaramäe from Estonia, who managed to catch up to me. At the foot of the descent, we made a 90-degree turn and all of a sudden had a huge tailwind.

Suddenly, we were just going warp-speed, and no one was going to catch us. And I eventually got a very satisfying victory. Afterward I remember my team leader, Frank Schleck, coming up to me and saying, "Wow, I didn't think that move would work for a split second! That was just stupid, absurd, and yet totally unbelievable. I've never seen anything like it. Straight uphill into the wind! How do you do that? You make it look so easy! Nobody thought you were going anywhere! I know you're strong and you're not stupid, but I wouldn't have bet a cent on that move to work!"

But you see, that's my trick. For 18 years, people always thought I was stupid and never believed in me, never thought my moves would last. You would have thought they might have figured it out at some point, but fortunately for me, they never did. There were always enough doubters to give me a chance.

Sometimes I got into a breakaway despite myself. Sometimes I didn't really want to be there, but I guess I couldn't help myself. Sometimes I just followed a move, and all of a sudden, I realized I was in the break again. I don't know if it's luck or instinct, but I got in a lot more breaks than I ever planned. And once you're in a breakaway and it's gone, well, you can't just sit up and say, "Oh, I'm sorry, fellas. I don't really want to be here!"

On a couple of occasions, I also got into a break without the love and support of my team directors. If you get yourself in that kind of situation, you'd better hope things work out well at the finish! Unfortunately, that is not always the case, and you pay the price for not following orders. Fair enough! But sometimes it all works out, and you go all the way and bring victory home for the team. On those days, you come off looking pretty good.

One of those days came with my win in the 2012 Tour of Colorado. That was one of the last victories in my career, but also one of my most satisfying. It was a short, mountainous stage from Aspen to Beaver Creek. It was a 155-kilometer stage, and straight out of Aspen, we attacked Independence Pass, which is one of the highest mountains we climbed the whole entire season. It's about 3,700 meters in altitude, much higher than anything we do in Europe. It's a killer 22-kilometer climb, and of course, attacks started immediately.

I was already way down in the overall standings, which is always good if you're looking for a stage win, so I went with the first group that broke away after only three or four kilometers. But the group was too big. There were more than 20 riders in the group, way too many to expect any real cooperation, because there were just too many different interests with the teams represented. Some teams were trying to drive the break, while others were trying to shut it down to protect the interests of their leaders back in the pack. I could see immediately that it was never going to work, that the break would just end up in a big yelling and screaming match. And behind, the pack was really chasing.

I'd already climbed over Independence Pass. I knew there were a couple of spots where the road actually leveled out and even dipped a bit before it started climbing again. So I waited for my moment. I sat last in the group going down this little dip. I even let a little gap open so that I could really build up speed. I started my attack at the bottom of this dip, and as soon as we hit the climb again, I just catapulted past everyone, about 10 kilometers per hour faster. It would have been impossible for anyone to get on my wheel and follow, and so, before you knew it, I had a 20-second gap.

But I still had 140 kilometers to go. It didn't really matter, though. I just knew that my best chance was to go alone. It was another one of those crystal-ball moments, where I could see everything play out before my eyes. I knew that the pack would likely let this 41-year-old go, because they wouldn't believe I could still go the distance. But I knew that if I crossed Independence Pass with a gap of one minute to one minute and 30 seconds, the pack would never see me again.

And that was pretty much what happened. But my team director, Lars Michaelsen, wasn't so sure. I remember that when he finally was able to pass the pack and come up behind me in the team car, he was nervous. He rolled down the window, and I could just see that he was looking for the right words to tell me that this was not a good idea. He didn't want to say something that would make me mad, but he wanted to make it clear that he didn't believe in this move. He was like, "Jens, you know, it's a long way to go."

Let's not forget that I was still climbing Independence Pass at over 3,000 meters of altitude. I didn't have a lot of oxygen for a heart-to-heart conversation, if you know what I mean. "I got a plan," I blurted out.

"Maybe you should wait for just a couple of riders, so that you have a little help?"

"No, no," I said. "I just need a minute over the top! Trust me. I feel good!"

Lars is an old teammate of mine. We raced together. We did some survival camps together. And yet he's younger than me. So Lars probably just said to himself, "Who am I to tell Jens what to do?"

From that point, he followed me and was really behind me 100 percent. I had a good one-minute, 30-second gap over the top and really attacked the downhill section. Behind, the race was all splintered up. I knew I just had to stay out front long enough until the pack regrouped. At that point, I knew that the leader's team would just settle into a pace and let me go, because I was so far down in the overall ranking. I knew that, once again, they would say, "Poof! Jens is 20 minutes down. He is no threat."

It took me forever to build up a two-minute lead, but once the peloton caught the remainder of the early breakaway, things got easier. I also got a boost once we hit the feed zone midway through the race, because I just blasted through it. I didn't slow down to get a musette bag of food or anything, as just about everyone in the pack did. As a result, I gained another 20 to 30 seconds.

Now there were times when it got pretty lonely out there. After all, 140 kilometers is a long way to go all by yourself. That's pretty much a four-hour solo breakaway, a long haul for just about anybody. But I was pushing and suffering too much to get bored.

Plus, believe it or not, there are a lot of things to keep in mind when you're in a long breakaway. You always have to remember to eat and drink regularly. I always try to stretch my back a little on the downhills just to loosen up a bit. But mostly, you just have to remain focused on the task at hand, which is maintaining your lead.

In moments like those, you only have your team director driving the support car behind you for company, and you really count on him. Lars was great. Once he saw that I was committed, he was, too. He kept driving up next to me to give me my time split, an energy gel, or a water bottle, and basically to encourage me. "Hey, you're looking good! You've got a two-minute gap now. You've got a three-minute gap now!" All those little details from a director really help keep you focused in a breakaway situation.

And then, at one point, Mother Nature helped out, because it started raining. I thought instantly, "This is good for me!" As I've learned over the years, anything sticky is good for me. I knew that back in the pack, the race would slow down as everybody dropped back to their team cars for a rain jacket and other gear. I just had on a short-sleeve jersey, but I knew I was working hard enough that my body would stay warm. I just said to myself, "I'M NOT SLOWING DOWN FOR ANY RAINDROPS HERE!" And I gained another minute on the pack, lengthening the gap to four minutes. With about 40 kilometers to go, the pack realized they weren't going to catch me and just eased up. I finished the stage with nearly a six-minute gap. Not bad for an old-timer!

Lars was just ecstatic. "That was so impressive," he said afterward. "But what was even more impressive was how daring you were to leave 20 riders behind so early in the race and just go it alone for 145 kilometers. Wow! Next time you can do whatever you want to do!"

We had a good laugh at that!

Cruising through Stage 7 during the 2013 Tour de France. (James Startt)

NEW HORIZONS

"Hey, you can only say 'Shut up, legs' to a point before your legs finally don't listen."

AFTER THE 2012 SEASON, I FELT REJUVENATED. The chaos of the season and the merger of Leopard and Radio Shack were behind us, and considering my results and my overall performance that year, I was confident that I still had at least another year in me. Trek also made it clear that they really wanted me to be a part of the team again. And like I said, as long as I was physically able to compete, retirement was simply not an option.

I still had concrete goals, too, like seeing Andy Schleck ride into Paris in yellow. After all, he'd finished second barely two years earlier. But things had gotten complicated for him in between, and I would realize this year that winning the Tour with Andy wasn't going to happen.

Problems started for Andy in 2012, when he had a bad crash in the time trial of the Dauphiné Critérium, a key warm-up race to the Tour de France. The Dauphiné is organized in the Alps and around the Rhone River Valley in French Provence. It's a beautiful region, but it often boasts high and powerful winds called Le Mistral. Anyway, Andy is a climber, a lightweight rider by nature. He came out of this village on a narrow road and got hit by a huge gust of wind that basically just picked him up and threw him down. The diagnosis revealed that he not only had a fractured hip but also a fractured pelvis, which proved to be very hard to heal, because whenever he would try to train, the muscles would pull on the fracture and it would open and close. It was immensely painful.

He missed the 2012 Tour and struggled to get back into shape. In what can only be considered a miracle, he came back and managed to finish 18th in the 2013 Tour. He started showing real signs of returning to form, but in hindsight, I think he made a mistake after the Tour. He should have gone straight into the Tour of Spain in September, because doing back-to-back stage races like that would have set him up for the next year. But he was tired after the Tour de France and didn't line up for the Tour of Spain, and soon enough, he lost the condition he had from the Tour and never really got it back.

When I look back on the Schleck brothers, Andy was more talented, but Frank was the harder worker. I have often seen that people with so much talent face an entirely different set of challenges than most of us humans. Because of their natural-born talent, things always come very easily for them, and it's easy for them to overlook the basic need to work hard. Some people are so talented that they can just skip training. Nobody finds out, because they're still very good in the races. I saw this with Jan Ullrich. He was just immensely talented but not always as focused as he needed to be. Sometimes, the most talented riders have it too easy. And when younger riders start coming up and challenging them, they're ill equipped to compete because they forget how to work hard. They forget how to accept defeat. Supertalented cyclists grow up suffering only when they're going for a win. And so when they find themselves suffering just to hang on, it's very hard for them to accept.

Suddenly, they can't get away with skipping training. Suddenly, if they haven't put in the miles over the winter, they're not just finishing second or third, but instead suffering just to stay in the peloton. And they can't wrap their heads around it.

That, my friends, is a luxury I have never known. I always had to work enormously hard just to make the cut. And I'm sure that helped me have a long career. Since I was never a great champion, my own physical decline wasn't as obvious as it would have been if I was a Tour de France winner. I never went from being a Tour winner or a classics winner to suddenly struggling to stay in the pack. That's a huge gap, and it must be incredibly humbling.

Often for the supertalented riders, cycling is more difficult on a mental level than it is on a physical one. These riders never needed to consider a plan B or a plan C before, because they had never experienced real difficulty or crisis. And when they're faced with having to do a month or two of hard training to get into shape, rather than, say, two weeks, they crack mentally.

But even though I went into the 2013 season quite motivated, I could sense that the end was nearing. For one thing, the numbers just weren't on my side. And I knew that at the age of 42, I couldn't keep pushing back the hands of time. I couldn't keep defying age, and I knew that age would one day defy me. It was getting harder for me to make the breakaways. It was getting harder for me to make the moves I wanted to make and needed to make to be a useful part of the team. Hey, you can only say "Shut up, legs" to a point before your legs finally don't listen.

But, mostly, it was getting harder for me to stay motivated to train.

My kids needed me at home more. Adriana, Kim, and Maya—my youngest girls—in particular, needed more help with their homework and all.

For the first time in my life, cycling became a job. For the first time, I was having trouble staying motivated for all the long hours alone on the bike that are required to remain competitive. Before, cycling had been pure fun, but now, part of it became a burden. The balance between the joy of riding and the suffering and sacrifice it requires shifted. I could feel it was the beginning of the end. It sounds dramatic, but that's exactly what I felt.

I still managed to have a good season in 2013, for what it's worth. It took me a long time to get in shape, but I won a great stage in the Tour of California and had a good Tour de France. Boy, that stage to Avila Beach in California may have been my last road victory, but it goes down as one of my most memorable. Still to this day, "Bling" (that's what we call Michael Matthews on Orica-GreenEdge) comes up to me and says, "Man, we still don't know how you pulled that off!"

And to be honest, I'm not sure, either. I was in a 25-rider group with no fewer than four Orica riders; three BMC riders, including my friends Thor Hushovd and Tejay van Garderen; plus Garmin had two or three riders. There was a lot of talent in that group. But I surprised them all, attacking on this little rise about 3.5 kilometers from the finish. I timed it just right and came by everybody just fast enough to catch them off guard.

But I was paying a higher and higher price for my efforts. For the first time in my life, I was falling asleep on the team bus after a race. And in the 2013 Tour de France, for the first time, I realized that I wasn't really dealing well with the stress of racing anymore. Risking your life on every downhill and constantly fighting for position are just a part of bike racing, but my tolerance for them was dwindling.

For much of the season, I was convinced that 2013 would be my last. But then I was good at the end of the season, and things were going really well with my team. We had great team spirit once again, and I was enjoying being a part of it. In addition, Trek was taking over as title sponsor, and they were very supportive of me. In August, I sat down with my team manager, Luca Guercilena, and he asked me, "Jens, should I reserve a spot for you on the team, or perhaps instead a director's position?" I thought about it for a second and said, "Luca, I think I still want to do one more year! I just don't feel like I should be in the car already next year. I still need to be a bike rider another year. I still need to suffer more before I can be happy with the decision to stop." So after discussing things with them, I decided to sign on for one more year. One final fling, as they say.

I also had a conference call with my mind, my body, my legs, and myself. And, basically, we came to an agreement. My body promised me that it could keep it together for one more year as long as I promised to release it from all the stress, suffering, and responsibility at the end of the year, because it was just going to fall apart after that. And I had to respect my body because, well, I surely didn't want it to fall apart in some big and beautiful bike race the following year with a million TV viewers around the world watching and realizing that I had raced one season too many!

But let me tell you, at the start of 2014, that's exactly what I was thinking. I was really regretting my decision to continue and really felt that I was in over my head, that I had signed up for that one infamous season too many. I remember calling Bobby Julich early in the year and saying, "Look, man, I think I did it. I think I'm doing one year too many. I'm not sure if I still have it. Heck, I don't even know if I want to have it anymore!" I was really struggling!

In the Tour of California, a race I had always done very well in, I wasn't even good enough to make the break most days. And on the final day, when I did actually make the break, I just wasn't good enough. I was in a break with Niki Terpstra, and at one point, he turned to me and said, "Come on, Jens, if we just go a little harder, we can make this work!"

I said, "Niki, I can't!"

He said "Ah, come on!"

At which point I blurted back, "Niki, you know me. I'm not tricking you. If I could go harder, I'd go harder. But I can't!" That was a very frustrating moment for me. Suddenly, I couldn't force a break to happen when I wanted to. I couldn't be Jens Voigt anymore.

This played out as much at home training as it did on the bike while racing.

Some days at home, I'd wake the kids up and get them ready for school. I'd make breakfast, get their teeth brushed, their hair straight, you know, the works. And then I would do the shuttle-to-school thing between the different schools.

But it wasn't until I got back home around 8:30 that the problem started. I'd sit there knowing I should just have another quick coffee and get on my bike like I'd done for 18 years. But, instead, I started finding a hundred reasons why I couldn't go ride right away. And the list of excuses just got longer and longer. You know, really important things. Maybe I should change a lightbulb. Maybe I should check my e-mail. Maybe I should fix this or that in the garage. After all, something surely needed fixing! No, the list continued on and on until one moment, I took stock of the situation and said, "Wait, Jens, you just don't wanna go out anymore. You don't like this enough anymore to make the daily sacrifices required!"

That's the moment when I knew that I'd reached the end of my career as a professional cyclist.

All those feelings, all the self-doubt, gave me the perspective needed to finally call an end to my career.

The Tour of California was a real wake-up call. I didn't want to finish my career like that! I knew then that something had to change. I knew that for the first time in my life, I wasn't working hard enough. So I went home and started working. I started getting out first thing in the morning again. By 9:30 at the latest, I was out the door. Screw the lightbulbs! They could be fixed later! I started focusing more on intervals and intensity in my training, the stuff that really hurts. I finally started getting in shape again.

A couple of weeks later, I went to the Dauphiné Critérium in France and was able to get into the breaks and make the moves. I knew then that I was good enough to ride one more Tour de France and tie the record of 17 Tours with Stuart O'Grady and George Hincapie, which only weeks before had seemed unimaginable.

In some ways, I actually had a better Tour than in 2013. I was recovering better. I wasn't falling asleep on the team bus like the year before. But, again, I realized that I no longer could tolerate the stress of the racing. And this was never more true than on the descents. I was good on the descents up to about 60 km/hr, not very fast, really. Between 60 and 80 km/hr, I was really out of my comfort zone. And anything over 80 km/hr, I was just like, "I don't want to be doing this anymore!" The idea of flying downhill with only a thin Lycra jersey and a helmet as protection just lost all its appeal to me! It was mentally very draining. It became obvious to me that this was going to be my last Tour.

Of course, there always comes that moment just after the race where you're feeling really good, that moment when you say to yourself, "Hey, that was pretty cool. I could do another one." And I did think for a moment that I could do one more and get the all-time record of 18 Tours. That moment lasted for about 30 seconds.

But while a lot of people talk about the Tour de France participation record, I was never really motivated by it. Hey, you don't get any flowers or special jerseys for participating in the Tour! It's true that it's a fitting honor for a rider who built his reputation on reliability to tie the record, but it was just not an honor that made me dream. I was always honored to be selected by my team to ride the Tour. That's always a big honor. But I was never motivated by the record. It's funny, because a lot of journalists wrote about it, and a lot of fans congratulated me for it. But for me, getting the record was more of a by-product than the achievement of a goal. Heck, I only learned about it when I started closing in on the record and people started asking me about it. The idea of breaking the record and going for 18 Tours was never a realistic option in my mind.

I had one more goal left before I retired, something that spoke to me much more than the Tour de France record. I was already preparing for the world hour record.

PREPARING FOR THE HOUR RECORD

"Look at the old Jensie! He's always good for a surprise! Who would have seen that coming?"

Jens as seen by Stéphane Gicquel (Voigt's physical therapist on Saxo Bank, Leopard Trek, Radio Shack, and Trek Factory Racing):

When Jens announced that he was going to attempt the hour record, he asked me to be there with him. I was originally scheduled to cover the Canadian Grand Prix races, but agreed instantly. Since 2009, I had been Jens's principal physical therapist, and I was honored because, well, only a handful of people get to work on such a project. And with Jens, I knew it would be a great moment, and I spent the weeks building up to the hour-record attempt with Jens at the velodrome in Switzerland.

Whenever you have a rider on the massage table, you have plenty of time to talk, and while preparing for the hour record, there was even more time. There was a sort of countdown as the record attempt approached, nine days until the record, eight days until the record. . . . But even though Jens knew that his career was inching ever closer to a close, the general tone of conversation was not one of nostalgia, but rather of satisfaction. Jens was satisfied knowing that he had won just about every race he was capable of winning. And he should have been satisfied. What young professional today would not be happy with a career as rich as Jens's?

But mostly, he was happy to finish his career on a high note. How many riders actually finish out their careers with a victory? Not many. But the world hour record is much more than a victory. Jens finished his career with a masterpiece!

SOMETIMES FRUSTRATION LEADS TO SUCCESS. That was definitely true of my situation in 2014, my last season as a professional. I was taking a real beating for much of the early season, as I was desperately trying to get into shape so I could finish my career with some dignity. The all-time low came at the Tour of California in May. I love that race and have always performed well in it, but in 2014, for the first time in my life, I wasn't strong enough to be where I wanted to be to make the moves. I was simply not good enough! The last thing I wanted after a 17-and-a-half-year career was for people to think I was just easing up and cruising in my last six months. I didn't want to slowly become invisible. No, I wanted to be competitive up until my last day on the bike.

I wanted to go out with my head up. More than that, I wanted to go out in style, in a memorable way. I wanted to find a unique way to entertain the fans one last time. Toward the end of the Tour of California, the International Cycling Union (UCI) sent out a press release modifying the rules for the world hour record, one of the sport's true landmarks. True to its name, the hour record measures the total distance a cyclist can cover on an indoor track in 1 hour. It is perhaps the ultimate test of a rider's endurance and his threshold for pain.

There had already been a lot of talk on the team about the hour record, because Fabian Cancellara was studying the possibility of making a run at it. He wasn't sure, though, if and when he would have the time to do it. But I saw that the rules had changed, allowing for a proper time trial track bike to be used.

Previously, the UCI's hour record rules had dictated the use of a standard frame with dropped handlebars and no disc wheels. When I read the rule changes, I thought to myself, "Hey, with these rules, I can do that!" The record at the time, held by Czech Ondrej Sosenka, was 49.7 kilometers (30.1 miles). I knew that, with the rule changes, I could beat that distance! I knew I could do something special. So I came up with this great idea, one that would make people say, "Look at the old Jensie! He's always good for a surprise! Who would have seen that coming?"

First I went to Tim Vanderjeugd, the team press officer, who is a good friend of mine. He liked the idea. Then I went to Jordan Roessingh, our tech specialist at Trek. I said, "Hey, Jordan, I have this idea to go for the hour record. What do you think? How far is Fabian along on his own attempt? Does he still want to do this? Is he committed? If he's not, then I'd like to step in." Jordan said that we could do some testing, and immediately I knew that it was the right thing to do. What a great way to finish out my career on a high note!

But just as suddenly, I thought, "Wait a minute. If I have this idea, there must be a thousand others who are thinking the same thing!" And there's so much work involved in such a project: finalizing the equipment, finding the best velodrome, and so on. The world hour record is a lot more than a simple 60-minute ride around a track. It's a huge undertaking! But still I was afraid that others would have the same idea, so we needed to move fast.

At first, I was thinking that I wouldn't be on the Tour de France team that year. That really wasn't my plan in 2014. Instead I thought that I might do a race like the Tour of Austria, which is a good week of hard racing, and then go straight onto the track for a month of intense track racing before attempting the hour record the first weekend after the Tour de France.

Before the Dauphiné Critérium in June, I flew to Brussels, and we drove to the Roubaix velodrome in France to do some testing. I was using my road time trial bike, but it was just for preliminary testing. We tested different helmets, skin suits, and wheel setups, and we started measuring how many watts I could do at different speeds. At the end of the day, things looked really good. The numbers led us to believe that I was in good enough condition to break the hour record, and from that point on, I had the green light.

Luca Guercilena, my team manager at Trek Factory Racing, got behind the project from the very beginning. Before taking over management of the team, he had been a performance trainer. He understood immediately that the hour record was a huge thing and that it could provide great visibility for the team. He understood the potential impact for both me and the team and wanted to help turn my attempt into a real event. And I'm thankful for that, because when I first came up with the idea, I just imagined I'd do it on some track with just a couple of people watching. I thought there would just be my dad helping me out with the day-to-day things—pumping up the tires and such—as he often did in the old days. Perhaps there would also be a couple of people from the team and, for verification, a UCI official. That's it. I honestly saw myself going for the hour record in an empty velodrome! But Luca knew better.

I was so excited by the idea that I really didn't care if I rode the Tour de France that year or not. Tying the record for the most Tour de France participations would have been nice, but it wasn't really much of a draw for me compared to the hour record.

I was fortunate enough to be in attendance when my old teammate and friend Chris Boardman broke the hour record at the end of his career. I'd always thought to myself, "Boy, what a great way to finish your career!" And now, suddenly, with the new rules, it was a real possibility for me, as well. Seeing Chris set the hour record was so exciting. I'll never forget it. It was up in Manchester at the velodrome, and the crowd was totally into it. They were just captivated by him and the event. Everybody was on their feet, giving him a standing ovation for the last 20 minutes. They could sense that it was going to be close for him to get the record, and they were totally going wild in support.

In addition, the hour record is such a beautiful event! The beauty of it lies in its simplicity. It's one bike, one rider, one gear. There are no tactics, no teammates, no bonus seconds at the finish. The hour record is just about how much pain you can handle! It's the hour of truth.

I'll never forget having breakfast with Chris the morning after he broke the record. He couldn't even walk! He was just in a world of pain! But it was hugely satisfying for him. It was a great way to finish a wonderful career!

But there was still so much to figure out. Where were we going to do it? How were we going to do it? We looked at a couple of velodromes. There was the track in Berlin and the one in Roubaix, but we finally settled on the Velodrome Suisse in Grenchen, Switzerland. It was new and fast. Plus, the people there wanted to work with us and gave us a lot of time on the track in preparation. Fabian lives about 30 kilometers from Grenchen and had already done some testing there. He knew the people that worked at the velodrome, and they were happy to have the exposure that an attempt on the record would provide.

You have to have a bit of luck to have a successful career for 18 years, and the timing of the UCI's rule changes was certainly fortuitous. I mean, if the UCI had changed the rules the year before or the year after my last year, the hour record would never have been a possibility for me. But suddenly it was, and it gave me the perfect objective to achieve and finish out my career in style. It gave me real focus to keep training and racing hard all the way up to the end. Suddenly, all the races had a new purpose, because in one way or another, they contributed to my hour record preparation. And after the beating I took in the Tour of California, it was nothing short of a dream come true! In the end, I did do the Tour de France, and it gave me a great base. Then I did the Tours of Utah and Colorado, which provided me with good altitude training before going to Grenchen for a month of intense training on the track.

I set up shop in Grenchen, a small town in western Switzerland, almost immediately upon returning to Europe from the States. There wasn't much going on in the town itself, but the velodrome was equipped with its own rooms and a small restaurant. So, from Monday to Friday each week, the Velodrome Suisse became my home away from home.

Training consisted of two 2-hour workouts each day. Luc Meersman, the father of Belgian pro Gianni Meersman, worked on our team and was there to help out with the day-to-day activities, as was my friend Stéphane Gicquel, who was the physical therapist I had worked with the most on the team. Then there was Jordan Roessingh, the technical director with our equipment sponsor Trek and Bontrager.

We also started working with Daniel Gisiger, a onetime amateur hour record holder. He works with the Swiss Cycling Federation at the Velodrome Suisse. Quickly, he became vital to our mission, as he is a real track specialist. Everyone else involved had a lot of road racing knowledge, but we lacked the in-depth track knowledge that Daniel possessed.

And then my team manager, Luca Guercilena, came up a lot. He was really curious to study all the preparation required for an hour record attempt. He was really involved. He wrote my training plan and oversaw some of my workouts. He gave me my time splits, analyzed my pedal stroke and my position, and did lactic acid tests. All are critical to succeeding in a 60-minute all-out effort.

You have to understand that getting ready for the hour record was nothing like getting ready for the Tour de France. The workouts were much shorter and more intense. Actually, what I was doing to prepare for the hour record was closer to what a prologue specialist might do when preparing for the short time trial that often marks the beginning of the big national tours. In the morning, we did an hour-and-a-half maximum on the track, but it was very, very intense. All the training was focused on maintaining an average speed of 50.5 kilometers an hour (31.4 mph), a time and pace that would allow me to beat the record, even allowing for a bike change, if I encountered a flat.

The hardest day of training was when I did eight 6-minute intervals from a standing start. I actually did that at 5 percent above the average speed, so I was hitting an average speed of about 51 kilometers an hour (31.7 mph). In addition, I barely had any recovery. I couldn't stop afterward. I had to maintain an active recovery, which meant that I would just get off my track bike, have a drink of water, and then put my road bike on rollers and spin my legs for a couple of minutes. The staff would also do a lactic acid test, which is important in an effort like the hour record, since you have to ride just under your lactic acid level. I had to change bikes for the recovery, because the gearing of my time trial bike was just too big. Rolling around easily just wasn't an option!

And, of course, just when I started to catch my breath, I would get the call to get ready to do another interval. After the fourth interval, I was just "buckled"! And on the fifth and sixth intervals, I really struggled to match my target time. But on the final two intervals, I could see the light at the end of the tunnel. I was pushing good watts, between 475 and 480, which was quite strong. During my hour record, I would have to average 412 watts, pedaling at 102 rpm. So knowing that, I was able to push on through with the final two intervals.

One thing we really had to focus on during training was the choice of gearing. We knew that at the end of 60 minutes, I was going to get tired, and it would be harder to push the same gear. Bogging down in the last 15 to 20 minutes was a real concern. I'm not Fabian Cancellara. He is amazing the way he can just spin a really big gear. I can't do that.

He can keep pedaling at 110 rpm for an entire hour. I can't. So we had to find a happy medium, and for me that was pedaling right around 100 rpm.

In the beginning, I was working with a 53 x 14 chain ring on the bike. But almost immediately, we realized that I needed to go up to a bigger gear, so we put on a 54 chain ring. After working with that for a while, Daniel Gisiger looked at me and said, "You know what? You still don't look like you're as efficient as you could be. We should try a 55-tooth chain ring." And that turned out to be the gear I used. In addition, I used longer, 177.5-millimeter cranks. They're harder to spin, but they provide better leverage for pushing big gears.

Daniel made a couple of other adjustments, too. He lowered my saddle just a little bit. He also suggested that I warm up with slightly smaller gears so I could spin more. In addition, he made me train with the black foam pads around the inside of the track that prevent you from slipping down. Those are in place during the official hour record, so he insisted that I start riding with them in place. He wanted me to get used to riding as close to them as possible without touching them, obviously.

He also insisted that, at the start, I stay out of my saddle for the entire first half of a lap, until I hit the second turn. That way, I got up to speed the fastest. But doing that is really hard, because it means that you're out of the saddle sprinting in the first turn. When you're starting at a standstill, you hit the first turn after only 25 to 30 meters, so you're nowhere near top speed yet. And it's really hard to maintain your balance on the steep turns when you're not up to speed. Heck, it took me three or four days of training before I actually managed to do a proper standing start! For the first few days, I'd get about two or three pedal strokes into the turn and then PANIC! I'd just sit down. Daniel was like, "Ah! Why did you do that?" But I just didn't have the courage. Somebody like Bradley Wiggins—someone with real track experience—would have laughed his head off at my pathetic attempt to become a track rider. Fortunately for me, I rode on the track a lot as a young amateur. That was always an important part of the East German sports school, so I wasn't a total novice. But it had been at least 15 years since I had been on a track, and track racing is a very different beast from road racing. To be honest, the last time I remember being on the track was in January 1998, just after signing my first contract with the GAN team. So there was a big learning curve for me to overcome.

The team really put a lot of science behind the effort. Trek dispatched a tech team to measure a lot of details. We had an apparatus on the track that would be triggered each lap when I crossed by. It measured the time and speed of the lap, and it would take a picture of me so I could study my position. It was very helpful. The hour record is all about consistency, but you'd be surprised by how much the data can vary from lap to lap. You think you're going the same speed; at least, that's the objective. But often there is quite a bit of variation. The guys from Trek really helped me even out my pacing to provide the most consistent performance.

In preparation for the attempt, I also had to live like a monk for an entire month. I had to be very careful about what I ate so that I didn't gain weight, because, while the training was intense, I was riding a lot less than when I was training on the road. That was tough, because after a season of road racing, I still had the appetite of a road racer. But I had to be careful not to gain weight. My afternoon workouts were mostly recovery. Most afternoons, I rode behind a scooter so I could spin my legs and recover from the intense morning workout. I was only riding about three hours per day, a lot less than I did on the road. In my downtime, I was just trying to recover so I would hang out relaxing in my room. About the only excitement I had that month was going out to get my hair cut or geocaching.

In the last week of training, some very special equipment arrived to give me that last little aerodynamic edge. Everything, of course, had to be approved by the UCI, but still my sponsors did everything they could to provide me with the most aerodynamic equipment that would be authorized. I had a special skin suit that zipped up the back. It took two people to get me into it. I had special gloves, special socks, you name it. You know, you can't just say, "Hey, I'm in good shape. I think I'll go for the hour record this week!" It just doesn't work that way. Massive organization is involved. It's a serious enterprise. My Trek team was behind me 100 percent. We left no stone unturned. And, soon enough, I was ready for the big day!

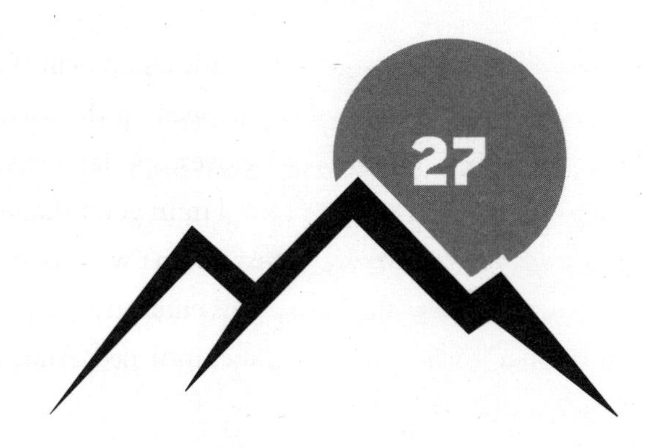

THE HOUR RECORD

"Everything I could physically feel was in pain."

MY BIG DAY, MY FINAL DAY AS A PROFESSIONAL, HAD ARRIVED. I couldn't have been more excited. Everything was set. We had figured that we needed to average of 18 seconds per lap. We had even trained for a bike change in case of a puncture, which took a total of 45 seconds, a little more than the time it would take to do two laps. We calculated what time we would let the public in, because a full house increases the temperature of the velodrome and also absorbs oxygen, which I needed a lot of that night.

Finally, we set everything around doing a 50.3-kilometer (31.25-mile) performance. I figured I could do that comfortably. And, mentally, the way my brain functions, it's better for me to know that I'm ahead of schedule rather that struggling just to stay on schedule. Some people function better with the added stress, but not me. I feed off positive motivation. And knowing that I was succeeding during the hour would be the best way to push me further.

In the morning, I did a short ride and a stretching session. Then in the afternoon, I just relaxed. Early in the evening, I went on the track and did a good warm-up ride. We let the crowd in at about 7:00 p.m., and I hit the track with Daniel Gisiger, riding behind his derny scooter. We did two 30-minute sessions. It was very relaxed, no stress. And then on the second one, we slowly built up the speed before I finally did the last two laps all-out by myself, just to prepare the body for what was coming up.

Then it was back to the locker room to towel off and get into the special skin suit and all the other special equipment.

I think it's safe to say that I was nervous. I was really excited, but yes, also nervous. I knew that after all my specific training and testing, I should have been able to break the record, but there's always that little bit of anxiety. After all, I knew that I wasn't as strong as I had been five or eight years before. Plus, things can always go wrong. You can have a puncture. You can start out too fast. You can just have a bad day. Hey, you can even have two punctures. If I'd learned one thing over the years, it was that nothing was a given in bicycle racing. And let's not forget that I was racing in front of a full house of fans. The Velodrome Suisse can seat 1,800 spectators. My parents were there. Bobby Julich was there. Jens Wichmann, one of the best men at my wedding, was there. Eurosport was broadcasting it in 75 countries to four to five million people, and more were following the stream online. So there was no place to hide. Of course, I was nervous. I felt the pressure, and I felt responsibility.

In the minutes before I started, I just tried to focus. I closed my eyes and focused on all the details that I had practiced the entire month before—my position, my breathing, staying on the black line. And while doing this, I was blocking out the crowd, the broadcast, everything. I couldn't let anything distract me. It was only when Daniel said, "Okay, Jens, one minute," that I opened my eyes again, took a deep breath, and stepped out onto the track and onto my bike.

As soon as the gun went off, I tried to focus my effort on getting up my cruising speed without building up too much lactic acid. Knowing how emotional I can be, I had to be careful not to go out too fast and end up in the red zone. That, too, was something we had practiced many times, and it was one of the points where I was probably most vulnerable. But after five or six minutes, I got a sense that I was on or possibly even ahead of schedule.

According to the UCI rules, I was not allowed to have a computer or any electronic apparatus that would allow me to see my progress. The only person allowed on the track was Daniel Gisiger. He had a whistle that he would blow on each lap when I should be crossing the start line. That worked out well, because despite all the people and all the cheering, I could always hear Daniel's whistle. I needed a point of reference, but it was important for me to keep it as low-tech as possible because I didn't have much time for analytical thought while I was out there! Mostly I just had to follow my body and monitor my breathing and pedal cadence to make sure I was in control of my effort. After a month of training, I had a pretty good idea of how my body felt at race effort.

I also compiled a little playlist that I rode to, to help push me along. I can't remember the entire playlist and didn't hear it half the time. But I do remember that I started with "Ready to Go" by Republica and finished with "The Final Countdown" by Europe. The playlist was very theme oriented, as every song had something to do with cycling or my last ride.

But I did hear the crowd. I understood later that they gave me a standing ovation for much of the hour, especially in the last 20 minutes. To be honest, I couldn't see them while I was out on the track, because it would have taken too much effort to move my head and turn it to the side. But I could hear them. And I could feel them!

I separated the attempt into three 20-minute segments. I knew I was ahead of schedule after the first 20 minutes and was worried that I might be going into the red, so I backed off a bit in the second 20 minutes. And then, in the last 20 minutes, I just really opened it up. By that point, I knew I was two-and-a-half or three laps ahead of the record, and I knew that I was in control and that I wasn't going to go into the red. And the last 10 minutes were all about blurring out and just giving everything I had left. By that point, my biggest concern wasn't the hour record, but the enormous saddle sore that was burning my butt! Everything I could physically feel was in pain.

With a few laps to go, I knew I had the record. Yet, I still went as hard as I could to raise the bar a little higher and to really give it all I had. There was no reason to hold back. This was it! This was the last race of my life, the last all-out effort I would do for the rest of my life.

Knowing I was going to have the record and I was going to retire in the fashion I wanted, I had a few instants to reflect on the moment. As you can imagine, the feeling was one of absolute, overwhelming emotion, one of pure joy and happiness. An absolute feeling of pride in knowing that I achieved what I wanted, that my last effort was worthwhile, and that the time, pain, and sacrifice were not a waste. But there and then, with four or five laps remaining, I also felt a tinge of sadness, because my days of performing in front of thousands of fans live, not to mention millions more on television, would be over the second the gun went off, signaling the end of the 60 minutes.

Already, in the middle of the most intense hour of my life, it hit me that a major life change was coming my way. But I pushed that thought back as far as I could. There was no time to wax philosophical here. Soon it would be a time to celebrate with my family and friends.

When the gun finally sounded, I instantly felt a burden lift from my shoulders. First there was the immediate burden of pain that I was in. There was just an immense sense of relief after racing for a full hour in that cramped-up position. Everything was aching. My neck ached from holding my head low in that aerodynamic position. My elbows hurt from holding my upper body in that position. My lungs hurt after burning and screaming for oxygen for so long. My heart hurt from the constant pounding. My back was on fire, and then there was my butt! I was really and truly in a world of pain.

But another burden also lifted: the burden of constant suffering, sacrifice, and stress; of training and racing hard; of risk taking; of missing my family; of chasing another contract for another year.

I must have had the biggest and happiest smile on my face for the next two laps, the time it took me to slow down, before landing in the arms of my teammates and parents. Everybody was smiling and hugging. It was a rare moment of pure happiness.

It was crazy. I ran across the track, jumped over the barriers, and started hugging random strangers. I was giving high fives and taking a million selfies with my fans.

Then we had the ceremony with UCI president Brian Cookson in which I was awarded a certificate saying that I was the official world-record holder. Me! Stupid little Jensie was the official UCI world-record holder!

After the anti-doping control, my team prepared a place where I could officially hang my bike up for good. I still have that photo of me putting my bike into retirement. Then I went back to my room and showered. Alone for the first time with no more soundtrack, no family, no team, fans, or cameras, I just sat on my bed for a while and let it all sink in. I just sat back as a steady stream of images flashed through my mind.

I thought about winning exactly 65 races. I thought about crashing at least 75 times. I thought about my 17 Tours de France. I thought about seeing some of my best friends succeeding and winning races. And I thought about losing my friend and teammate Wouter Weylandt in a fatal crash.

I won a lot of races in my career, but I lost far more. Still, I always knew I was in a lucky position to turn my passion into my profession. And now, at 43, I was closing the largest chapter of my life. Something

I'd done passionately for 33 years had come to an end. Getting out of the shower, I looked at myself in the mirror for a second and just thought, "Okay, I will never be this fit, strong, skinny, and well trained for the rest of my life, never ever! It's only downhill now." I just passed the highest point of my physical strengh and fitness. I will never, ever be Tour de France fit again, period! That was hard to swallow.

But, again, there was happiness and pride, because I finished my career on a high note. I finished my career with the support of my friends, family, and team. And I finished it on my own terms, which I knew was critical to my peace of mind moving forward.

Knowing what I know today, I probably backed off too much in the middle 20 minutes of the record. Chris Boardman once said, regarding the hour record, "If it's easy to hold your speed, then you're going too slow." And in the middle section, I would say I played it too conservatively. But I was still just ecstatic once I crossed the line. What a great night. What a great event. What a great way to end a career!

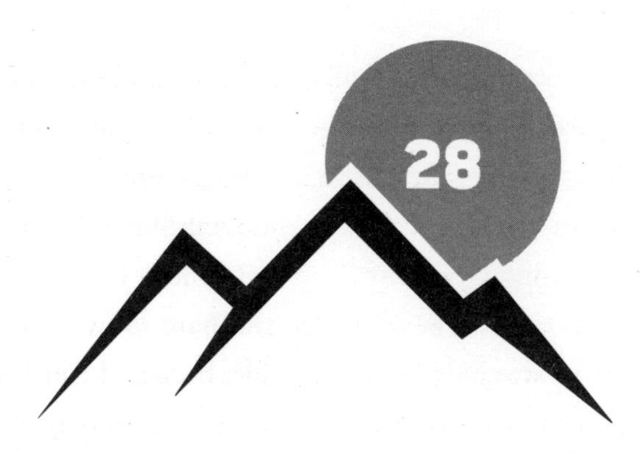

LIFE AFTER CYCLING

"Don't cry because it's over;
smile because it happened."

I MAY HAVE HAD AN ENTIRE YEAR TO GET MY HEAD AROUND THE IDEA THAT I WAS RETIRING, A WHOLE YEAR TO PREPARE. Still, though, there were plenty of surprises. I guess in my naive little world, I thought that I would have more time to relax and do the things I hadn't really been able to do much as a cyclist. Finally, I thought, my life as a fisherman could start! I could just see myself sitting on the banks of one of Berlin's many lakes every other day. And after 33 years of cycling, yes, I thought I deserved at least some time to relax.

But, that didn't happen, and soon I found myself traveling as much as when I was racing. First off, since I knew that I would retire after the 2014 season, I had fielded quite a few requests and offers to do things like charity rides and gran fondos and other such events. And knowing that I would have more spare time, I agreed to many, always saying, "Yeah, I want to do that. Let's plan it after the 2014 season!" So, when my season and career came to an end, I sat down and wrote down all the rendezvous and appointments I had agreed to. I had charity rides in England and Luxembourg; Trek Travel in California; gran fondos in Germany; a trip to Perth, Australia; and a team training camp in Spain. The list was just unending!

Fortunately, at least, I like to travel. And now that I'm no longer a professional cyclist always focused on racing, I can actually enjoy the places I travel to. I can actually do something called sightseeing! I'm no longer obliged to stay in my hotel to conserve energy.

When I woke up jet-lagged at four in the morning at the Tour of California in 2015, I didn't need to stay in bed and try to sleep. Instead, I just brushed my teeth, went out for a walk, and did a little geocaching. I just enjoyed the nice, quiet streets in the early hours of the morning.

In the Tour Down Under I actually had time to visit the Adelaide Zoo, where I got to see their brand-new panda bear space. As an active cyclist, the idea of walking around a zoo for hours is just unthinkable.

And then, of course, there was the fact that I didn't have to wake up every morning and think, "Okay, what's my training program today?" That alone was a huge change after 33 years.

But the changes were both good and bad. It was great not to have to think about how many intervals I was going to do, and it was great not to have to ride in the rain. But what was not so great was the lack of purpose. For the first time in my life, I didn't actually *have* to get out of bed at all!

I worked hard to avoid falling into that famous hole that so many others told me about after they stopped their own careers. It's a universal problem. It doesn't matter if you're a car mechanic, an opera singer, or an athlete. If you've been doing something passionately for a long time, there's going to be a big void in your life whenever it is that you call it quits.

It's challenging, and I must admit that I did struggle at first. There were new emotions, new thoughts, new projects, and the unknown. What helped me there was having a great and functioning family with strong bonds. My wife and my children helped me to survive this initial period of struggle. They were always there to listen to my thoughts and my problems. There were days when I felt as if someone had amputated a limb from my body, like I wasn't whole anymore. There were days when I thought retirement was the biggest and best invention ever made by humans. There were days when I wondered why I hadn't retired earlier. There were days when I felt empty without cycling. It was a real mixed bag of emotions. And while it was great not to have the obligation to train, it was clear that I needed new objectives.

In the first year after retirement, I basically told myself that I would accept any job offer that came along, be it a charity ride, TV commentating, blog writing, working as an ambassador for races such as the Tour Down Under or the Tour of California, or working with Trek bicycles in some way. And then, of course, I had this book to finish!

Believe it or not, I never had a manager throughout my whole career. But now, more than ever, I needed one. So, for the first time in my life, I have a management company, and that really helped me transition into a "normal" life.

And it has been good! I was a really experienced bike rider, but suddenly, I was confronted with a need for new and different skills. And I was struggling. So I reached out to people who were able to help me get my new life started. And so far, it's working out well. I've learned a bunch of business things, corporate things, and legal things. And I've learned how to deal with my new freedom and my new life.

I've only just realized the obvious, that there is life beyond cycling, a whole new world outside of being a professional athlete. And now more than ever, I'm excited to see where my future takes me.

I made an appearance to help raise money for stem cell research in Germany. I did the Tour de Cure in Australia to help raise money to fight cancer. I've been involved with the Soldier On veterans organization.

I've been working with ASO, the Tour de France organizer, to have greater involvement in women's racing at the Tour de France. And I've been working with my business partner here in Germany to further develop the Shut Up, Legs brand.

And I'm also very excited to have passed the tests so I can be a team director. Many of my old teammates are a lot less excited by that possibility, though, because they're scared that I'll be too hard on them. My Spanish friend and longtime teammate, Markel Irizar, joked about my being a director by saying, "Jens will tell us to chase down a break or close a gap, but if we can't do it, he'll just start yelling, 'What? Are you kidding me? I did that for 20 years all alone! Do you want me to get out of the car right now and show you how it's done?'" We all had a good laugh at that one.

But actually, my teammates shouldn't be worried. I've been getting practice with my son Julian, who has been racing. And I have to say that when I'm not racing myself, I can be pretty relaxed at the races.

Last but not least, I've been keeping busy with my six children, who are happy to finally have Daddy around. And just in case they don't keep me busy, my wife, Stephanie, has a to-do list that stretches from Berlin to Paris. So there are plenty of things to occupy my time and attention.

But life as a fisherman will still have to wait. And what happened to my dream of buying a motorbike and driving all over Europe for three months with no plan, no schedule, just getting out on the road and enjoying the trip? Or my idea of going fishing five out of every ten days? Or that childhood dream of spending one winter in Alaska or Canada in a wooden cabin, living off the land and being totally disconnected from TV, the Internet, and smartphones while making my way through 50 books? Or horseback riding in Patagonia in southern Argentina? Or seeing the Calgary Stampede, Yellowstone National Park, Hadrian's Wall and the Scottish Highlands and Cape Wrath,

Transvaal and Kruger National Park, or the Great Barrier Reef? I've got so many ideas and dreams left to chase, and I have not given up on them. I still want to make them all come true.

The challenge of being a responsible family man and still chasing my dreams continues for me. There are still so many adventures ahead, and surely I will explore and learn new things and laugh and cry and struggle and fail and get back onto my feet, raising my six children, and I guess pretty soon my first grandchildren. My life will challenge me, and I will challenge life. So far, I have no reason to complain at all. If my life continues in the interesting way it has until now, I will die a happy man.

By far the most horrifying aspect about retirement for me was the idea of losing the fitness level I'd achieved as an elite athlete. Nowadays, I huff and puff when I carry a basket of clothes from the basement to the bedrooms upstairs. I realize, "Damn, I wasn't like this before!" That realization is very painful, accepting the fact that I am, in fact, mortal. After all, during all my years as a cyclist, my job was to not be normal. I was paid to do things that were not human. Coming to terms with the new, mortal Jens has been the biggest struggle in my retirement by far.

But on the bright side, Stephanie prefers me a little chunkier, and she's perfectly happy with the idea that her husband doesn't look like some emaciated skeleton anymore. And since I love to eat, it's been easy to maintain my new chunky image with her.

I'm right now at my winter weight, the weight my body was trying to get to every winter, around 82 kg (180 pounds). I would start the season around 78 kg (172 pounds) and go down in the season to 77 (170 pounds) or even 76 kg (167.5 pounds) in the Tour. So with 5 kg more than race weight, I'm happy, but I don't want to put on any more weight. At my age, putting on weight is like concrete. Once it's there, it's really hard to get rid of! Plus, I'm still trying to be a good example for my kids, so I don't want them to see their dad getting all fat and lazy, right?! But I'm not going to get fat anytime soon. I'm still very busy, just like I was as an active rider.

And when I do look back, I'm the first to say that my sport has been really good to me, and if somehow I found myself at the start of my journey again, I wouldn't change too many things about my experience.

It was, of course, not always a pleasure cruise for me. I still have a titanium screw in my left hand and steel and titanium in my right hand. I've suffered three broken collarbones and endured surgery on my right shoulder to repair ruptured ligaments. About 25 nails and screws have been used in my body. I've had 11 broken bones, about 120 stitches, and lost probably half a square meter's worth of skin in all my crashes, 75 in all. I rode just a little less than 900,000 kilometers on my bike over the course of my career, a distance equivalent to traveling up to the moon, back down to Earth, and then again a good portion back up to the moon. Just saying. I missed the birth of my son Julian because it was during the Tour de France. I missed many of my children's birthday parties. I hardly ever was at home for my wife's birthdays, and after missing my plane because of terrible traffic in Paris, I "celebrated" my 30th birthday all alone in an airport hotel in Paris.

But none of that stopped me from loving my sport and putting all the passion I had into it. I learned lessons for life, met great people, made many good friends, met my wife, had the chance to race and ride in close to 40 countries, and experienced many different cultures and religions. Cycling helped me to broaden my horizons, to be open-minded, curious, and ready to learn new things every day. The fans became a large part of my life, which is a reason why I continued racing and continued to travel the world as I got older.

One thing I'm already looking forward to is becoming a granddad. That will be so awesome, and I will spoil my grandkids badly. And when I get to babysit my grandchild one day, I will build him or her a slingshot, take the child into my kid's garden, and say, "Here, my grandchild, is a slingshot. Here is a little rock to use as ammunition. Over there is the neighbor's window. And now Granddad is going to turn around and not watch you anymore." And then, when I hear the neighbor's window break, I'm going to say, "Okay, now you run back to Mom and Dad." Oh, how I love that idea! Maybe I'll have another book to write 15 years from now, and that story will be in there.

But first I need to finish my transition to a more normal life, my career after my career. And as I said before retirement: Don't cry because it's over; smile because it happened.

Fishing . . . I thought I would have more time for this once my career was over. I'm not the most patient person in the world. But if my success rate does not improve, I may have to resort to dynamite. (James Startt)

I would have been nowhere without my family—they are my heroes and my loved ones. They gave me the chance to explore the world and more important they kept me grounded. I would not have been half the man that I am now without them. They have been on my side in good times and helped me through the hard times.(Courtesy of Jens Voigt)

Acknowledgments

I WANT TO TAKE THE CHANCE TO THANK A FEW PEOPLE WHO HAVE BEEN IMPORTANT IN MY LIFE.

Starting, of course, with my family—my wife, Stephanie, and my children, Marc, Julian, Adriana, Kim Helena, Maya, and Helen, and my parents, Egon and Edith Voigt. And, of course, I can't forget my brother, Ronny, and my sister, Cornelia. Nobody can achieve anything without the strong support and love of a family, not to mention parents teaching you the right things as a child.

Cycling gave me the chance to meet some really great friends: Stuart O'Grady, Chris Boardmen, Bobby Julich, and the Schleck brothers. Thank you, guys, simply for being my friends.

Thor Hushovd and Jens Wichman, two of my oldest friends and the best men at my wedding, also hold a very special place in my life.

I would never have had such a long career without my three childhood coaches, the Eichberg brothers. One taught me to ride correctly, one taught me discipline and dedication, and one taught me how to suffer and how to go fast.

My grandma Frieda Voigt always believed in me and was my first "sponsor" when I lived as a junior in the dormitories at the sports school in Berlin, providing me with a much-needed 50 East-German Marks per month to help me get by in the big city.

My amateur coach in Berlin, Dieter Stein, was also crucial in my formative years and somehow a real father for me in Berlin.

And, of course, my four professional team directors, Heiko Salzwedel, Roger Legeay, Bjarne Riis, and Luca Guercilena, played key roles in my career, as well as being friends, mentors, and leaders.

I would also like to thank Trek Bikes for being such a cool and great partner in the last 5 years of my career, for becoming my friends, and for organizing the best-ever sendoff into retirement in cycling history with that special bike design and cycling outfit. And let's not forget the amazing support they gave me for the hour record project.

And most important, I want to thank all my loyal fans and supporters who were standing behind me all those years, believing in me, and supporting me.

Jens Voigt

No major book can be tackled alone and *Shut Up Legs!* is no exception. I am greatly indebted to many of my editors at *Bicycling* magazine, especially Peter Flax and Bill Strickland, who promoted the online diaries with Jens that provided the groundwork for this book.

I am also indebted to Mark Weistein at Rodale Books who allowed us to take the idea into a full-book form. He, along with his team, were tremendous in the editing process.

My parents, James and Cathy Startt, have provided a bed of support and encouragement over the years, and the sense of historical perspective, so crucial to my father, has come in handy on every book project I have done.

I always hold a special place in my heart for Samuel Abt, nothing short of my mentor. His many books on cycling defined the genre, and his ever-astute eye was a godsend at different points in the making of this book.

My wife, Rebekah, and my daughter, Ella, have always provided the best reason to get off the road and come home, and Ella is already an experienced hand on the Tour de France.

I am also greatly indebted to many people who were part of Jens Voigt's amazing journey and am grateful for their input, many of which were included in certain chapters. Thank you, Jan Schaffrath, Samuel Abt, Roger Legeay, Chris Boardman, Thor Hushovd, Sébastien Hinault, Heiko Salzwedel, Francis Bur, Stuart O'Grady, Chris Anker-Sørensen, Bobby Julich, Lars Michaelsen, and Stéphane Gicquel.

And, last, I am grateful to Jens. In my more than 25 years covering the Tour, his story stands alone. Thank you for allowing me to help tell it!

James Startt

The dynamic duo in a rare down moment.

About the Authors

JENS VOIGT is a German former professional road bicycle racer for several teams, the last one being UCI ProTeam Trek Factory Racing. Voigt competed in the Tour de France a record-tying 17 times and twice wore its famed yellow jersey, though he never challenged to capture the overall title. His career achievements include winning the Critérium International 5 times and a number of one-week stage races, as well as three Tour de France stage victories. In September 2014, he set a new hour record. He lives in Berlin.

JAMES STARTT is an American photographer and writer based in Paris. The European associate of *Peloton* magazine, he has covered more than 25 Tours de France and published the first English history of the great race, *Tour de France/Tour de Force.*

Index

Boldface page references indicate photographs. An asterisk (*) indicates that photographs appear in the color insert pages.

A

B

C

D

E

J

K

L

M

N

O

P

Q

R

S

T

U

V

W

Z